Nell

Island under siege

The U.S. blockade of Cuba

By Pedro Prada

OCEAN PRESS

Cover graphic by José Ortega (courtesy of International Peace for Cuba Appeal)

Cover design by David Spratt

Copyright © 1995 Pedro Prada
Copyright © 1995 Ocean Press

All rights reserved. No part of this publication may be reproduced, stored in a retrieval system or transmitted in any form or by any means, electronic, mechanical, photocopying, recording or otherwise, without the prior permission of the publisher.

ISBN 1-875284-88-5

First printed 1995

Printed by Australian Print Group,
Maryborough, Vic.

Published by Ocean Press,
GPO Box 3279, Melbourne, Victoria 3001, Australia

Distributed in the United States by the Talman Company,
131 Spring Street, New York, NY 10012, USA
Distributed in Britain and Europe by Central Books,
99 Wallis Road, London E9 5LN, Britain
Distributed in Australia by Astam Books,
57-61 John Street, Leichhardt, NSW 2040, Australia
Distributed in Cuba and Latin America by Ocean Press,
Apartado 686, C.P. 11300, Havana, Cuba

Contents

Publisher's note   1

A brief history   3

Island under siege   7

Impact of the blockade   31
by Roberto Robaina, Cuban Foreign Minister

Questions and answers about the blockade   46

Appendices

Kennedy, Cuba and cigars   *by Pierre Salinger*   50

UN Resolution 47/19 on the U.S. blockade against Cuba
Approved by the General Assembly November 24, 1992   51

Resolution of the European Parliament on the "Cuban Democracy Act" *December 1992*   52

Testimony to 1994 U.S. Congressional hearings on Cuba policy
by Wayne Smith   53

Report from the American Public Health Association on health in Cuba   55

Opponents of the blockade   57

❖

The United States has used many different pretexts [for not lifting the blockade and normalizing relations]. At one time, when we were in Africa, they used to say if the Cubans withdrew from Africa, then relations would improve.... They said that when links with the Soviet Union were cut off, then our relations would begin with the United States. Now the Soviet Union is not supporting us anymore and nothing has changed. They keep moving the goalposts... Before it was Latin American subversion, the situation in Central America... and when they talk about "reforms" in Cuba, it is a precondition that we cannot accept because it has to do with independence and the sovereignty of our nation....

I wish I were the problem. But the problem is the revolution, and the problem is our ideas. The United States, or some people in the United States, do not just want Castro's retirement. They want the total destruction of the revolution. And that is what the majority of Cubans will not accept....

FIDEL CASTRO
From interview with Marvin Shankin Cigar Aficionado, *Summer 1994*

Publisher's note

In this book we present a brief outline of the issues and history of the 32-year U.S. blockade against the island nation of Cuba. Since the 1959 revolution, nine U.S. presidents have pursued a policy designed to starve the Cuban people into submission.

While Washington insists on describing its trade and travel ban on Cuba as an embargo, the character and effect of the extensive U.S. legislation, in reality, amounts to a blockade. We have therefore accepted this definition in this book.

The U.S. blockade against Cuba has increasingly developed an extraterritorial reach, as President Bush bluntly stated in April 1992: "My government will continue to press governments around the world on the need to isolate economically, the Castro regime. Together we will bring to Cuba a new era of freedom and democracy."

Nevertheless, this strategy has been questioned by editorials in major U.S. newspapers, such as the *New York Times*, the *Washington Post*, and the *Wall Street Journal*. It has also been widely condemned by the international community, most recently by the United Nations General Assembly in November 1992 and again in November 1993, when 88 countries voted against the U.S. blockade, with only four countries in favor and 57 abstentions. This issue is scheduled for review at the 1994 session of the UN General Assembly.

As appendices we have presented a partial list of international figures opposed to the U.S. blockade, the 1992 UN Resolution ("On the need to put an end to the economic, commercial and financial embargo against Cuba imposed by the United States"), and the resolution of the European Parliament on the so-called Cuban Democracy Act of 1992.

Other materials included as appendices illustrate the range of U.S. opponents of the blockade, including Wayne Smith, former head of the U.S. Interests Section in Havana during the Carter presidency, and the report of the 1993 fact-finding visit to Cuba by the American Public Health Association.

❖❖❖

We would like to acknowledge the assistance provided by: Diane Atkinson for translation; José Ortega and the International Peace for Cuba Appeal for permission to use the cover graphic; the Center for Cuban Studies in New York for the valuable contribution made by its publication *CUBA Update*; Mirta Muñiz of the Ocean Press office in Havana for coordinating the preparation of sections of this book; and Wayne Smith, Mike Krinsky and the American Public Health Association for permission to reprint statements on the blockade. Finally, this book would not have come about if not for the initiative and enthusiasm of Pedro Prada, one of Cuba's youthful and talented journalists, now an adviser to Cuban Foreign Minister Roberto Robaina.

All quotes contained in this book are retranslated from the original Spanish-language manuscript.

Deborah Shnookal
September 1994

Recommended reading

The Cuban revolution and the United States: A chronological history. By Jane Franklin. 1992. Ocean Press with the Center for Cuban Studies. 276 pp.
Cruel and unusual punishment. The U.S. blockade against Cuba. By Mary Murray. 1993. Ocean Press with the Cuba Information Project. 117 pp.
United States economic measures against Cuba: Proceedings in the United Nations and international law issues. Richard Falk, Michael Krinsky and David Golove. 1993. Aletheia Press
Blockade: U.S. policy of siege against Cuba. Reference materials. 1993. New Magazine Publishing Co. (Toronto). 66 pp.
CUBA Update: "The time has come to end the embargo against Cuba." Vol 3, 1994. Center for Cuban Studies. 28 pp.

PRESIDENT THEODORE ROOSEVELT
Letter to Henry White, September 13, 1906

Just at the moment I'm so angry with that infernal little Cuban Republic that I would like to wipe its people off the face of the earth. All that we wanted of them was that they should behave themselves and be prosperous and happy so that we would not have to interfere. And now, lo and behold, they have started an utterly unjustifiable and pointless revolution and may get things into such a snarl that we have no alternative save to intervene — which will at once convince the suspicious idiots in South America that we do wish to intervene after all...

A brief history

January 1, 1959
   The U.S.-backed military dictatorship collapses. Batista flees Cuba as revolutionary forces led by Fidel Castro begin to take power.

July 3, 1960
   U.S. import quotas on Cuban sugar are reduced.

October 19, 1960
   The U.S. government declares a partial embargo, prohibiting exports to Cuba except for non-subsidized foodstuffs and medicines. Cuba proceeds to socialize wholesale and retail trade that had been U.S. owned and also nationalizes Cuban-owned businesses.

January 3, 1961
   Washington breaks diplomatic and consular relations with Cuba.

April 17, 1961
   An invasion force, secretly sponsored and financed by the U.S. government, invades Cuba at Playa Girón (Bay of Pigs) and is

defeated within 72 hours. Later, it is disclosed that the CIA began in early 1959 to organize activities against the Cuban government both inside and outside the island, including attempts to assassinate Fidel Castro and other Cuban leaders, sabotage, armed attacks from both air and sea, and assaults on Cuban diplomats abroad.

September 1961

The U.S. Congress prohibits all assistance to the Cuban government and authorizes the President to establish and maintain a blockade on all commerce between the United States and Cuba.

January 31, 1962

The Organization of American States votes to exclude Cuba from the organization, and an arms embargo against Cuba is imposed.

February 3, 1962

The U.S. government imposes a total embargo of U.S. trade with Cuba, except for the non-subsidized sale of food and medicines.

September 4, 1962

Latin American Free Trade Association votes to exclude Cuba by a vote of 7 to 4 with Mexico and Brazil abstaining.

October 2, 1962

The U.S. government sends cables to all Latin American governments and NATO countries outlining new measures to tighten the global embargo.

October 18, 1962

U.S. Commerce Secretary Hodges issues the following announcement: "Close all U.S. ports to ships that carry any supplies to Cuba, when on the same continuous voyage, they attempt also to dock or take on cargo in the United States."

October 23, 1962

CIA writes a memorandum on the "effect on Cuba of a blockade covering all goods except food and medicines." It concludes that such a blockade, in and of itself, "would be unlikely to bring the Castro government down unless it were extended over many months."

1964

Members of the OAS are called upon to prohibit trade with Cuba.

May 1966

The House Agricultural Committee votes 16 to 3 for a $3.3 billion "Food for Freedom" bill that includes a prohibition on food aid to any country engaged in trade with Cuba or North Vietnam.

September 1, 1977

Cuba and the United States under President Carter open Interest Sections in the two countries. This represents the first diplomatic presence of Cuba and the United States in Washington and Havana since January 3, 1961.

September 28, 1977
Castro says Cuba would be willing to discuss payment of compensation as demanded by some U.S. companies as long as the United States is willing to compensate the damage the blockade has caused the Cuban economy. He stresses Cuba's desire to develop peaceful relations but cautions that Cuba will not compromise its principles.

June 19, 1979
Rep. Ted Weiss (D-NY) introduces unsuccessful legislation to end the U.S. trade blockade against Cuba and to re-establish diplomatic relations.

October 4, 1983
President Reagan signs the Radio Broadcasting to Cuba Act initiating "Radio Martí."

1986
The U.S. Commerce Department passes a "Parts and Components Rule." This new regulation allows U.S. subsidiaries and foreign companies to export goods to Cuba without applying for a licence if the goods contain less than 10% U.S.-origin materials and are valued at less than $10,000.

August 23, 1988
President Reagan signs into law a Trade Act initiated by Rep. Howard Berman that eliminates restrictions on imports and exports of books, films, phonograph records and other informational material to and from Cuba.

October 26, 1990
Congress passes a trade bill that includes the Mack Amendment (sponsored by Senator Connie Mack, R-FL) that would make it unlawful for subsidiaries of U.S. companies in foreign countries to trade with Cuba, even in goods of local origin.

February 5, 1992
Rep. Torricelli (D-NJ) proposes a bill to extend and tighten the blockade. Among its features, the bill ends U.S. corporate subsidiary trade with Cuba (70% of which is in foods and medicines), calls on the President to pressure Western allies to enforce the blockade, sanctions Latin American countries that trade with Cuba, prohibits any ship that trades at a Cuban port from entering a U.S. port in the next six months, and allows the funding of opposition groups on and

off the island. The Torricelli law, known as the "Cuban Democracy Act," is passed through Congress in September, 1992.

November 24, 1992
The United Nations General Assembly votes for a resolution, "On the need to put an end to the economic, commercial and financial embargo against Cuba imposed by the United States." Fifty-nine countries support the resolution, three (the United States, Israel and Romania) vote against it, and 71 abstain.

May 1993
H.R. 2229, the "Free Trade with Cuba" bill, is introduced by Rep. Charles Rangel (D-NY). First hearings on the bill are held March 17, 1994. Rangel proposes the removal of all restrictions on trade, including those on foreign subsidiaries of U.S. companies, on investment, travel, and telecommunications. The unrestricted sale or donation of food and medicines would also be allowed.

November 3, 1993
The United Nations General Assembly passes another resolution urging the United States to end the trade blockade. Eighty-eight countries support the resolution, only four (the U.S.A., Israel, Paraguay, and Albania) oppose it, with 57 abstentions.

FACTS ABOUT THE U.S. BLOCKADE AGAINST CUBA

The blockade prohibits:

- Exporting all U.S. goods to Cuba, including medicines and foodstuffs
- Importing any Cuban goods to the United States, including food and medicines
- All other types of commercial activity between the two countries
- Imports of third country products that contain Cuban materials
- Travel to Cuba for U.S. citizens except for official, journalistic, special professional or family purposes
- Third country ships visiting Cuba from docking in U.S. ports
- Open trade between Cuba and U.S. subsidiaries

Island under siege

✧

Although I do not recall the exact date, during a schoolyard discussion one day, while we happily enjoyed the wisdom that we all imagined we had at some stage between childhood and adolescence, someone echoing his father praised Leyland buses as the best in the world. Another, no less "well-informed," stated: "Listen, the Americans bought Leyland from the English so that they wouldn't sell buses to Cuba."

This was my first awareness of the blockade against my country, and I associate it with another more recent and dramatic illustration — that of a friend who constantly faces death. The journalist Elder Santiesteban has no kidneys and lives by dialysis. We frequently suffer the desperation of seeing him in intensive care, clinging to the life that threatens to leave him, while doctors struggle with the defective dialysis machines from the Argentinian Medix firm, to whom the U.S. Treasury Department denied a licence to sell spare parts to Cuba.

For a reader accustomed to the term embargo, the word blockade could sound harsh, or perhaps inappropriate. As a Cuban who lives under its ominous shadow, I see how the blockade affects the millions of people who live on our island and those who have left, young and old.

That is why I can only describe it as one of the first and most long-lasting low-intensity conflicts initiated by the United States. There have been moments of truce, dependent on conditions dictated by the East-West conflict, the Cold War and the existence of the Soviet Union and a community of socialist states.

There have also been skirmishes, ambushes and counterattacks disguised by a dense forest of laws designed to make a siege look like an embargo, even as a protective action by the U.S. administration to save Cuba which, according to United Nations statistics, was the most prosperous country of Latin America.

However, these statistics hide what U.S. Treasury Department sources have revealed that during the last years of the 1950s, U.S. companies in Cuba received a net profit of 329 million pesos (at that time equivalent to $329 million). Some 84 percent of this was transferred to the United States. This exploitation was so blatant that President Kennedy was later to observe: "We know perfectly well what happened in Cuba, for the misfortune of all. I believe that there is no other country, including those in Africa and others under colonial domination, where there has been more humiliation and exploitation than in Cuba, in part attributable to the policies of my country during the Batista regime."

When the political and economic relationship between the two countries changed after the 1959 revolution, Washington chose a bland and neutral term to camouflage its policy of aggression against Cuba. Thus the blockade appears as a legal measure in response to a failure to pay compensation, or a civil or military crime — using the withholding of money or goods as means of economic and political pressure against a country that supposedly represents a threat to international security.

The embargo became part of the legislative framework — and is still subordinate to it today — of the Trading with the Enemy Act, which implies both a hostile state and a declaration of war. Instead, what we have is a country that in no way threatens the supposed victim, violates no norm of international coexistence, and presents no challenge to world peace and security. The sanctions that have been applied are based on the fundamental legal tenets of the Cold War.

For Cubans, the embargo is nothing more than a euphemism that hides the fact that the blockade's purpose is to place the island under siege. The blockade aims to exhaust Cuba's resources, in order to force the civilian population to surrender. The restraining forces of the Cold War — the Soviet Union and the socialist camp — have been defeated. What remains in today's unipolar world is the blockade in its crudest form, attempting to encircle a tiny Caribbean island.

Blockade or embargo

To clarify the question of blockade or embargo, I took advantage of the opportunity to speak to Dr Olga Miranda Bravo, Vice-President of the Cuban Society of International Law and member of the International Court of Justice in the Hague.

Having studied the issue over more than 20 years, Dr Miranda argues that the blockade transcends the status of an embargo because of the existence of an incredible abundance of legislation that forms the legal scaffolding that supports the U.S. blockade imposed against Cuba.

"It cannot be considered an embargo — as they publicly maintain — because Cuba is not indebted to the United States, nor has it committed a crime so punitive to justify the seizure and destruction of its assets by the United States. With these measures, they have pursued a policy of asphyxiation and isolation of Cuba in order to cripple it, a policy of war being applied against Cuba in a time of peace," said Dr Miranda.

"The Naval Conference of London in 1909 established as international law that a blockade is an act of war. This principle was invoked in 1916 by the United States itself in order to assert that no foreign power had the right to obstruct the exercize of free trade by non-involved countries, imposing a blockade when no state of war has been declared."

Nevertheless, for a long time it was said that the complaints about the nationalizations that took place in Cuba in the 1960s were sufficient grounds for maintaining the blockade. A lobby of companies that were affected by these nationalizations, the Joint Corporate Committee on Cuban Claims, demanded compensation to the order of $1.8 billion plus a further 6 percent in interest payments — which almost doubled the original figure.

The government of Fidel Castro had already committed itself to comply with Article 38 of the 1940 Cuban constitution, which stipulated that compensation for expropriations be paid in 20-year fixed-term government bonds with an annual interest rate of 4.5 percent.

On this point Olga Miranda commented: "The government of Cuba has always been prepared to discuss its differences with the United States on an equal footing. In February 1960 the Cuban Foreign Ministry made this known to the U.S. government. However, the reply unfortunately reflected traditional big stick diplomacy, demanding 'prompt, adequate and effective compensation' from Cuba, a principle long abolished in international relations."

"As to global compensation," Dr Miranda continued, "the form that post-war conventions have tended to adopt, is a lump sum agreement. This involves diplomatic negotiations between governments which lead to the fixing of the amount of compensation paid over several years and distributed to the interested parties by the government that represents them."

As it happened, Cuba did pay compensation to property owners and to the governments of Great Britain, France, Canada, Italy, Sweden, Mexico and Spain. Because of this, Dr Miranda concluded, it is clear that the United States does not want to negotiate to defend the interests of its citizens, as other countries have done. For 35 years successive administrations have denied the rights of U.S. citizens who had properties in Cuba, solely to maintain the blockade.

How does the United States sustain its policy on Cuba? Are U.S. citizens really aware of the actions of their government?

In an 8 to 1 judgement on March 23, 1964, the U.S. Supreme Court stated: "Every sovereign State is obliged to respect the independence of each and every other sovereign state and the courts of a country must not judge the actions of the government of another country when they are carried out within that country's own territory. Any compensation for damages caused by these actions must be obtained via channels that allow each country to exercize its sovereign powers..."

And it added: "Despite the grievous effect that an expropriation of this type can have on the public norms of this country and the states that compose it, we came to the conclusion that both in the national interest, and in the interests of the practice of international law between nations, it would be better to maintain the doctrine of the Act of Sovereign Power intact so that it is adhered to in this case."

This verdict was overruled by the Foreign Aid law of 1964 which classified the Cuban nationalizations as being contrary to international law since there was no compensation, ignoring Cuba's compensation law (no. 861) of July 6, 1960.

Global operation

The first steps toward of the blockade began in 1959, incited by ultra-conservative journalists and by United States officials who had had close links with the deposed regime, and who recommended taking a tough stand against the new revolutionary government. For example, Richard Nixon, who later came to be president, had maintained relations with the dictator Fulgencio Batista since the 1950s.

At the end of August 1959, the American Foreign Power Company announced the cancellation of loans worth $15 million which had already been promised, after the Cuban government reduced by 30 percent the rates paid for electricity to the Cuban Electric Company, which was owned by the U.S. corporation.

On October 14, 1960, the *Wall Street Journal* made its first public announcement of the blockade, the first phase of which was implemented a week later. The Law of Congress No. 3447 signed by Kennedy on February 3, 1962, completed the process.

In its present form, what Washington calls the embargo has been based on various pretexts, depending on the moment: First, it was the nationalization of land and other social measures; then it was the expropriation of U.S. businesses and the "unpaid" compensation; later, it became the alliance with Moscow, "subversion" in Latin America, the support to national liberation movements in Africa; then the Cuban refusal to apply reforms similar to those of Soviet perestroika and now "the lack of democracy and respect for human rights."

All of this underlines Washington's consistent policy of seeking to crush all Cuban dissent and independence, a policy pursued even more vigorously over the last 35 years under pressure from those who wish to re-establish Cuba's pre-1959 economic and political dependency.

Those sectors of Cuban society, defeated by the revolution and now living in the United States, have taken the "Cuba question" out of the arena of international relations and placed it on the domestic agenda. Since 1981 the Cuban American National Foundation has obtained some $200 million to finance the political and economic war against Cuba.

This is the reason why the dispute between Washington and Havana today has very little to do with philosophical or ideological doctrines, and much less with the previous East-West conflict. It reflects the commitment that was made when the first 250,000 Cubans emigrated in 1959. Those Cuban emigres represented the most powerful section of the Cuban economy and included many of those who had been involved in the tortures and crimes of the dictatorship. Today, even some in conservative circles in the United States say that Cuba could become a strong regional economic power using its low-cost but highly-skilled labor force and reactivate its economic potential, which they recognize that while it may be paralysed today, was built after 1958.

So, the blockade left Cuba without raw materials and spare parts. Factories were idled, so that mothers like mine had to cut up cotton sheets to make underwear for their children.

Cuba was thus obliged to look further afield in its search for trading partners, given that its natural trading partner, with obvious geographical, cultural and historical ties, was now off limits. Cuba has sometimes been criticized for having developed one of the biggest merchant shipping fleets in the Third World. But there were not many alternatives. Produce and raw materials for the consumer market and for Cuban industry had to come from Europe and Asia.

When I revisited Cuba last February [1993] ... I discovered pediatricians at otherwise splendid hospitals who spend every morning counting scarce medications for the children... the director of a day care center dreaded that the milk supply would dry up for her preschoolers, as it has for all Cuban children older than 7... How should we feel about an embargo that is keeping food and medicines from Cuban children? I feel ashamed.

Dr Benjamin Spock
From a letter to the New York Times, *June 3, 1993*

BLOCKADE: COST TO CUBA

U.S.-Cuba trade was over $1 billion a year before 1959. Since then the blockade has cost Cuba an estimated $38-40 billion in both lost trade as well as extra costs in importing products from other countries.

With the collapse of the socialist trade block, Cuba's imports were drastically reduced by two-thirds. Cuba's only option was to increase trade with the West.

In 1992, 70% of Cuba's trade with U.S. subsidiary companies was in food and medicine, accounting for 15% of its imports (valued at $533 million in 1990). This trade was banned under the Torricelli law (Cuban Democracy Act) in violation of international law and United Nations resolutions that food and medicine cannot be used as weapons in international conflicts.

...This misnamed act [the Cuban Democracy Act] is dubious in theory, cruel in its potential practice and ignoble in its election-year expediency.... An influential faction of the Cuban American community clamors for sticking it to a wounded regime....There is, finally, something indecent about vociferous exiles living safely in Miami prescribing more pain for their poorer cousins.

NEW YORK TIMES Editorial: "Making poor Cubans suffer more."
June 15, 1992

On top of the blockade came a series of economic attacks. When pig production began to take off in Cuba in the 1970s, a sudden attack of swine fever forced us to slaughter millions of animals and establish rigid health measures and other restrictions, causing damages amounting to $10 million.

Something very similar happened when in 1981 dengue fever caused dozens of deaths, obliging Cuba to search the world for methods of combating mosquitoes, while the transnational pharmaceutical companies and their subsidiaries were forbidden to sell us the pesticide malathion. Their operations in the Caribbean and Latin America were closely monitored to enforce the blockade. As a consequence, my country suffered losses of around $100 million.

Carlos Batista, a researcher for the Centre for U.S. Studies in Havana, considers that there have been other epidemics that have been part of this economic war. These include the red mildew which attacked the sugar cane, destroying plantations in 1988, with damages of $220 million; the coffee mildew in 1990 that cost more than $41 million; and blue tobacco mold in 1988, which caused nearly $350 million in losses.

These actions against Cuba contrast sharply with the way that money from the United States was poured into those distorted and dependent Caribbean and Latin American "model" economies which are today described as "economic miracles." In order to demonstrate the superiority of the "free capitalist market" over the "centralised orthodox communist market," the United States propped up these economies through the various Latin American and Caribbean Basin initiatives.

Over more than three decades the blockade produced other distortions such as the dependence of the Cuban economy on the Soviets and Eastern Europe. That was why, when the Berlin Wall fell in 1989 and Vice-President George Bush announced to Ronald Reagan that the Cold War had ended and that the United States had won, it was firmly believed that Cuba would be the next to go under.

While awaiting the death blow to Castro, the ultrarightist elements among Cuban emigres in alliance with conservative Republicans launched a legislative maneuver which was hoped would lead to an internal revolt against the Cuban government. The Florida Senators Bob Graham and Connie Mack each presented draft legislation in the Spring of 1990 which was subsequently accepted, to become part of U.S. trade law.

The Mack Amendment, as it is known, was approved by Congress in October 1990. It sought to prohibit all trade with Cuba by subsidiaries of U.S. companies located outside the United States; to impede the granting of licences for any type of trade with Cuba; and it proposed sanctions or cessation of aid to any country that bought sugar or other products from Cuba.

The firm opposition of Washington's allies who protested any U.S. measure which violated their free trade or affected businesses under their legal jurisdiction obliged President Bush to allow the deadline for signing the law to expire and to apply the so-called pocket veto.

After the disappearance of the socialist countries of Eastern Europe and the Soviet Union, Cuba could no longer be considered as anyone's "satellite." Cuba lost the source of 80 percent of its supplies and its biggest market. The island was forced to go through the second major restructuring of its economy in a very brief and traumatic period.

Thus, it was expected that Cuba would be incapable of overcoming this tremendous test and many thought that the best course of action was to widen and deepen the siege, to make it more international so as to use poverty to pressure Cuba to acquiesce. Enter Representative Robert Torricelli.

A president as political hostage

Torricelli arose out of the shadows of the Mack Amendment, which was put aside in 1990 by the then leader George Bush following severe warnings from its Western partners.

Torricelli was a beneficiary of the Cuban American National Foundation, and he would be insignificant without that support. Young, with desperate political ambitions and ultraconservative thinking, it was through Torricelli that a sector of Cuban emigres hoped to achieve power within the American Union. It was the vindication of an electoral alliance between the ultraright lobby in Miami and the Republican and Democratic parties.

The so-called Torricelli Bill [passed in 1992] proposed restricting trade by United States subsidiaries with Cuba, reducing the Cuban people's access to many essential foods and medicines. At the time, precisely 70 percent of these subsidiaries' trade with Cuba was in foods and medicines. It should be noted that when an embargo was applied to Iraq during the Gulf War, the government of the United States exempted foods and medicines for humanitarian reasons.

There is sufficient evidence to accept the claims that Congressman Torricelli was strongly pressured by an extremist sector within the Cuban American community — a sector which is often presented as the only voice within this national group. However, today the primary concern of most members of this community is the survival of their family members on the island. The Torricelli law has only increased the suffering of Cubans on both sides of the Florida Straits.

Torricelli received $56,000 from the Cuban American National Foundation, raised by very doubtful methods with help from Cuban American businessman Jorge Mas Canosa. Those familiar with the way politics are played in the United States, will consider this quite a cheap price.

The Democrats needed votes to get Clinton into power and Bush wanted a reelection at all costs. Despite the fact that the General Assembly of the United Nations had approved a resolution (47/19) entitled "The need to put an end to the economic, commercial and financial embargo against Cuba by the United States," leaving Washington isolated in the voting, Bush put his signature to the document that Bill Clinton had earlier endorsed in an effort to win the state of Florida.

That was how a piece of legislation which was patched together, came to be passed — despite the many reservations, congressional disputes, criticisms and warnings by Washington's allies, editorial reflections and commentaries by major newspapers and a substantial rejection by the world community. Bernard Aronson, then Undersecretary of State for Inter-American Affairs, did not hestitate to admit: "The Cuban Democracy Act is not a change of policy. . . It promotes the political and economic isolation of Cuba. We are doing that and we have been doing that for more than 30 years."

Despite what happened in the United Nations, the U.S. government decided to go outside international law, violating resolutions 47/19, 38/197, 39/210, 40/185, 42/173, 44/215 and 46/210 of the highest world body, the General Assembly. Similarly ignored was the decision of the Tenth Summit of Heads of State and Government of the Nonaligned Countries Movement which condemned the blockade and its extraterritorial application and described it as a tool of war.

A plethora of restrictions

For Andrew Zimbalist, economics professor at Connecticut's Smith College, "The present policy of the United States against Cuba is an anachronism, it is inconsistent and counterproductive; it is marked by the escalating economic war that the Cuban Democracy Act launched in 1992 and supported by the Bush and Clinton administrations. . . By increasing Cuban dependency on the capitalist market, the prolonged

U.S. embargo becomes more costly than ever. . . . Cuban efforts to engage in free trade with the capitalist world are being blocked not only by the inadequacies in the way they conduct business with the United States but [especially] by the [U.S.] efforts to stop Cuban trade with companies of third countries."

Today all trade with subsidiaries of U.S. companies in third countries has been totally frozen. Between 1988 and 1989 this trade rose from $246 million to $332 million, and reached $705 million to $718 million between 1990 and 1991. To achieve that, the subsidiaries had to go through a crippling bureaucratic process, expose themselves to numerous legal risks and sometimes operate through intermediaries, in an undercover way, despite the fact that 300 licences had been granted.

All this is no longer possible. Researchers from the John Hopkins University in Washington have calculated the damage to their country's trade at some $30 billion dollars and the annual losses to businesses at $750 million a year.

In 1993 the news that the Cuban government had authorized the use of dollars by Cuban citizens caused a sensation. Until then the use of the U.S. dollar had been restricted to certain commercial operations and Cubans working outside of the country. However, now that the Cuban government has removed the internal restrictions, the dollar continues to be a prohibited currency — prohibited by the U.S. government.

U.S. citizens, for example, are prevented from traveling to Cuba because they are prohibited from using their own country's currency there. They are thereby forbidden to have any physical, visual or cultural contact with Cuban society. In this sense, their cultural and human rights are violated. This same policy prevented Sydney Pollack and Robert Redford from filming *Havana* in Cuba and demands that doctors, religious persons, scientists and journalists who travel to the island for some very special reason, account for all their expenditure, which must not exceed $100 a day.

Such travelers are also told that they cannot see their families and friends, and that any expenditure above the fixed limit must be declared. If the travelers are of Cuban origin they must comply with special regulations about buying Cuban goods and bringing their purchases back to U.S. territory. Many emigres encounter enormous difficulties when they try to send even small amounts of money to their families in Cuba as economic and humanitarian aid.

In practice, the U.S. federal authorities do not openly prohibit travel to Cuba, as this would not be politically palatable. Instead, they create all sorts of obstacles, including for Cubans residing in the United

States. They make traveling complicated, they alter flights and timetables, they control the amount of money that can be spent and stop the use of credit cards. And all because, according to the *Miami Herald*, Cuba would receive some $100 million annually from these trips — a figure Cuban authorities consider to be an exaggeration.

Those who make it have to put up with a host of prohibitions: you cannot bring back literature, papers, music or souvenirs from Cuba. Medea Benjamin, executive director of Global Exchange, a foundation that has campaigned for freedom of travel and which in 1993 and 1994 led groups that violated the travel ban to Cuba, told the *Miami Herald* of the bitter experience of returning to her country: "They seized our passports. They developed our photographic films. They confiscated our videos, books, magazines, journals and articles, all of which are supposedly protected by the first amendment to the constitution. They took a sweater off a child of 14 because it said 'Cuba awaits you'. . . For exercising our constitutional right to travel, we are in danger of receiving sentences of up to 10 years of loss of liberty and fines of up to $250,000. In effect, the United States is the only western country where traveling is a crime. . ."

As a result of these challenges, there is a move to lift the travel ban to Cuba, which has won support within sections of the Administration. But President Clinton is still bending to pressure from the anti-Castro emigres to stop its signing, which would be a blow to the political lobby in Miami.

The blockade affects the ties among separated families whose only option is communication by telephone. Each year 40 million calls between the United States and Cuba are attempted, but only 400,000 can be made because of the limited number of lines available. There are 143 telephone circuits in the depths of the ocean that are "under embargo." Their reopening would mean an income of $27 million in 1994 for AT&T alone. Cuban specialists have voluntarily made minor repairs to these ancient underwater cables, but Cuba is not in a financial or technological position to repair or replace them.

Cuba's payment for its part of the telephone service is frozen in U.S. banks, although the amount due is disputed. If this money were recovered, then together with the profits of a fully functioning telephone service, there would be enough income to provide a huge boost to the Cuban telecommunications industry. For many families it would bring great happiness and the rights of millions of people would be restored.

In fact, the blockade violates 12 articles of the Universal Declaration of Human Rights, including the rights of those U.S. citizens who have protested their government's anti-Cuba policy only to find their names and photographs ending up in FBI files.

In Miami, terrorism is openly practised. One of the most insidious episodes was the destruction of the painting *El pavo real*, by the Cuban painter Manuel Mendive, which was considered a classic of Cuban art. In 1993, Americas Watch denounced the repeated violations of freedom of expression, and the political and physical repression that is used against anyone in Florida who dares to oppose the right-wing sector of the Cuban community and speaks up against the blockade.

According to the FBI, in Dade County at the end of the 1980s there were attempted bombings against the Cubanacan, Machi Viajes a Cuba and Marazul Charters travel agencies. Similar actions were directed at the Spanish Grocery Store, the Museum of Cuban Art and Culture, the Institute for Cuban Studies in Miami, the medicine and package courier agencies Cubaenvios, Va Cuba, Miami Cuba, Bele Cuba Express; the private houses of María Cristina Herrera, director of the Institute of Cuban Studies in Miami, Ramón Cernuda, director of the Cuban Museum of Art and Culture, Griselda Hidalgo, who supports unrestricted commerce with Cuba; and radio station WQBA-AM for publicizing the attack on the house of María Herrera.

No-one is prepared to stop such actions because the government itself encourages them. U.S. businesses participating in two conferences sponsored by the British firm Euromoney, dedicated to promoting business opportunities in Cuba, have been closely monitored by the Treasury Department, the FBI and the CIA. Several international tenders for rights to explore for and extract petroleum in Cuban territory have had to put up with a lobby of diplomats and supposed journalists who warn them that these territories are U.S. properties.

In November 1993, the *Washington Times* reported how the former U.S. ambassador to Honduras constantly worked to try to stop any commercial, political or diplomatic contact between Cuba and that country. Also, at the beginning of 1994, Britain's *Financial Times* reported that U.S. government officials had warned off businessmen who were interested in investing in Cuba.

"These warnings," said an unidentified official of the United States, "have been delivered not only to countries of the Caribbean, but also especially to Europe, Canada and Latin America... We cannot say to people that they must not invest in Cuba, but we are warning them that when the political and economic situation in Cuba changes, the true owners of the property will want to recover their goods or receive significant compensation. Some will want both."

So apparently the owners of Cuba are not those persons who work there, live there and defend their country! Such an attitude was insulting not only to Cubans but also to the foreign businessperson, who happened to be a Mexican who sold $40,000 worth of personal hygiene products to Cubanacan. An official of the U.S. embassy in Mexico introduced himself at a luncheon to recommend that the Mexican should review his business since it would be better to sell $1.5 million worth of goods to the southern states of the United States than to sell two containers of goods to Havana.

The blockade has a long history. There are lengthy testimonies of how even non-U.S. companies have been obliged to rescind contracts, withdraw credit and not to fulfill contracts, using the most incredible excuses. The most recent cases have been with tour operators and hotel chains interested in the Cuban tourist market.

One of the best examples was the case of the Spanish company Tabacalera, investor and cosponsor of the Cayo Coco tourist project in the north of Cuba. Despite the goodwill of many people and the growing interest in the Cuban tourist trade and the benefits of investing in Cuba, Tabacalera was threatened with bankruptcy and had to withdraw. Finally, Guitart Hotels took over the project and brought it to fruition in 1993, overcoming enormous pressures.

Sometimes, the restrictions lead to ridiculous situations, such as happened during the CNN coverage of the visit of Mikhail Gorbachev to Cuba in 1989. In the studio in the luxurious Havana Libre Hotel, a CNN official who probably had instructions from the U.S. Treasury Department, took great trouble to destroy the video cassettes that would not be taken back to Atlanta, so that Cuba could not use them.

During the 1991 PanAmerican Games in Havana, all sorts of obstacles were put in the way of the ABC network paying Cuba for transmission rights. Hewlett Packard, which has provided the drug testing certificates for the International Olympic Committee for all international sporting competitions during the last decade, also suffered the same problems. So did Coca Cola, during the World Athletics Cup in Havana in 1992, an event which the firm had traditionally sponsored.

Trade under attack

Stuck to the glass on many of the doors of the Ministry for Foreign Trade in Havana, there are still some stickers from the 1960s that warn staff and visitors: "Careful. The enemy is listening..." That may seem paranoid, but not so. Thanks to the intelligence operations that Washington uses to pursue Cuban trade, businesspeople on the island have been obliged to carry out their work with a high degree of confidentiality, sometimes as actual undercover operations. Fidel Castro has described how an antitoxic medicine controlled by the United States was obtained surreptitiously in order to save the life of the young man Rolando Pérez Quintosa.

The whole world has been led to believe that Cuba does not engage in trade because it is entirely subsidized. This ignores the trade that has taken place between Cuba and the rest of the world for the last 35 years; it assumes Cuba had no products, raw materials or equipment to trade, to pay for its industrial and individual consumption. These stories provide a covert smokescreen for the police-like activities that representatives of the U.S. government use throughout the world to undermine Cuban trade, and which have always been directed primarily against the most important imports and exports for Cuba: that is, sugar, nickel and petroleum. Before the official passage of the blockade in 1962 there were already many restrictive measures in place, such as the lowering of the Cuban sugar quota in the U.S. market. Today, efforts are directed at discouraging those who want to invest in tourism and other branches of the Cuban economy, and limiting Cuba's access to international markets.

María de la Luz B'Hamel, of the European and North American department of the Cuban Ministry for Foreign Trade, described how between 1980 and 1983 the United States government imposed agreements upon important Cuban nickel buyers such as Italy, France, Japan, Germany and Holland, forcing them to certify that none of their exports to the United States contained even an ounce of Cuban nickel.

"The Soviet opposition to this treaty led to the United States suspending the purchase of any Soviet nickel products from 1983 until November 1991, when the former Soviet Union agreed to the contract," she explained. All of these accords are still current.

Similarly, importers of Cuban sugar had to use independent warehouses so as not to violate the certifications that accompany their sale to the biggest world buyer. Canada, for example, is obliged to maintain independent silos, offices and workers to handle Cuban sugar, since it is the main trading partner of the United States.

This happens with all other exports and with all those who trade with Cuba. The U.S. Treasury Department periodically circulates lists of companies linked with Cuba. In 1989 alone, eight such lists were produced. They not only included legally established commercial firms in third countries, but also individuals, banking and shipping entities. These lists are designed to harass businesses and persons subject to U.S. laws, who are prohibited from having any relation with those blacklisted. This violates the principle of free trade, which the United States hypocritically proclaims. The lists are accompanied by a memorandum that resembles a criminal file. Fines of $50,000 and/or 10 years in prison await anyone who ignores those instructions.

As well as the lists, any commercial operation involving Cuba is monitored with the intention of trying to halt it. I have witnessed the anguish of our businesspeople when they have managed to negotiate some deal for Cuba, only to have the contract broken soon afterwards, or what is even worse, to find the doors closed, even if the deal involved humanitarian products such as medicines.

Medicuba, the Cuban firm that imports medicines and health technology, has had numerous experiences like this. In just one year, Medicuba had to pay an extra $45 million for pharmaceuticals, including drugs vital to testing for fetal abnormalities and for cardiovascular irregularities.

According to the list prices, Cuba often pays 80 to 140 percent more than other buyers of medicines, medical technologies or equipment from such firms as Sigma or Talgrex International Export.

Not even books are beyond the reach of the blockade. In 1989, there was a case similar to that of the Leyland buses. The McGraw Hill publishing house acquired shares in the Spanish firm Editorial Interamericana from whom Cuba had traditionally bought specialized publications on medicine and therapeutic techniques. They then refused to sell these books to Cuba, resulting in a lack of up-to-date scientific and medical literature for Cuban doctors and scientists.

Medicuba has frequently tried to buy medicines to alleviate asthma or to counteract diabetes, or to combat an epidemic, only to confront a restricted market that excludes everything that is under U.S. jurisdiction, control, or influence.

In general, trade is distant and dispersed, so that freight costs are very expensive. Add to that the impossibility of receiving the financial benefits that go to other countries and the obligation to pay in currency other than dollars due to the restrictions against Cuba.

Work at the offices of Medicuba is often tense. On one occasion, there was a severe shortage of Salbutamol for asthma. There was none in the country's pharmacies and very little in the hospitals. Every attempt to buy a shipment and bring it to Cuba was thwarted. Finally, after many attempts, a substantial shipment was loaded on to Cubana airlines in Europe.

Unfortunately, this is not an isolated case. In Cuba there are 16.5 diabetics per thousand inhabitants. The Elli Lilly Co. monopolizes the world production of insulin and regulates its prices. On more than one occasion Cuban diabetics, including children, have been on the verge of death, because of the refusal to sell Cuba this medicine, even through third or fourth countries or as a humanitarian gesture. Cuba has been forced to locate it thousands of kilometers away.

At the same time, we find that Cuba has developed one of the most promising pharmaceutical and biotechnological industries of the Third World, only to do daily battle in order to place its highly competitive and sometimes exclusive products on the markets controlled by the multinationals.

"Surrender, meningitis B!" was the headline used by the Argentinian paper *Pagina 12* to celebrate the end of the battle to gain entry for the Cuban vaccine Va-Men-Goc, the only one in the world that could prevent that type of meningitis. Apparently, Argentinian authorities and scientists were faced with all sorts of pressures from the United States to impede its acquisition, even after hundreds of people had died.

The importation of foodstuffs is a similar story. In 1991, in Moscow I saw Leonor Domínguez, a Cuban representative of Alimport, cry from rage and frustration when her contract for baby food was broken as soon as the then U.S. Secretary of State James Baker passed through the Soviet capital. At the same time, the agreements that other firms had made to buy Cuban sugar were annulled when the persons who had authorized them disappeared mysteriously from the Soviet enterprises concerned.

Alimport, a Cuban firm in charge of importing food, has been one of the main victims of the Torricelli law of 1992. In that year alone, some $40 million extra had to be spent on freight to buy frozen chickens. A year later, the difficulties in guaranteeing the transportation of products became even greater. To cite an example, in 1993 as an immediate consequence of the law, there were serious delays in the arrival of priority products such as soya flour (used for chickens) and milk for children.

In both cases the problem was one of transportation. The soya flour had been purchased but could not be brought to Cuba because the effects of the Torricelli Bill made it hard to contract shipping companies. The result was a shortage of eggs and a huge number of chickens had to be killed because they had not reached commercial size and the farmers could not afford to feed them.

In another case, a very high quality shipment of milk was purchased at a very good price but then could not be transported. The contract had to be renegotiated. This involved tying up funds in letters of credit for the original contract, as well as additional resources for the new one.

The implications of the Torricelli law were explained by Mauricio Fernández, an official of the Cuban Merchant Shipping Fleet, as follows: "A ship that visits a Cuban port cannot visit the United States for six months afterwards. The United States is the biggest world market, followed by Europe. Which ship owner wants to tie up its ships for six months just to take a shipment to Cuba? To find a ship to come to Cuba is neither easy nor cheap."

The effects of the blockade

Feeling the pressure of the sanctions that have been imposed, Cuba maintains that today it should have the right to claim compensation for damages caused to the Cuban economy by the so-called embargo, its host of restrictions and the effects of U.S. military and economic aggression. According to the Cuban expert on the blockade, researcher and journalist Nicanor León Cotayo, Cuba has suffered greater losses due to the blockade in 30 years than the equivalent to a whole year's normal work throughout Cuba. It is also equal to the expenditure required to supply Cuba with the necessary quantity of soaps and fats until the beginning of the next century.

The most recent calculation of losses due to the blockade, according to the Cuban Vice-President Carlos Lage, is $40 billion. But that may not take into consideration all losses, such as lost investments or investments under less favorable terms.

There are also damages that cannot be calculated, such as measures to protect the environment that require huge financial and technological resources which are denied to Cuba. One example is the contamination of Havana Bay, which is one of the 10 most damaged in the world. The damage to the marine ecosystem is significant, but it is even more tragic that our ability to save it has been greatly reduced by the credit barriers we face and by the refusal to sell the technologies and the biological decontaminating detergents that are controlled by U.S. monopolies.

Immersed in our daily activities, we Cubans sometimes forget the noose that has been placed around our necks, while others use it to justify many errors, including administrative and economic inefficiencies, and bureaucratic and commercial obstacles. For Silvio Rodríguez, singer and recently elected member of the Cuban National Assembly for Batabanó, these attitudes make it harder to confront the blockade and constitute "a third blockade" — the first being that imposed by the United States, and the second being the collapse of trade with the socialist states.

This "third blockade," Rodríguez says, would include some Cubans who are crushed by pessimism and inertia, genuine bureaucrats who always moan: "It can't be done," "We don't have the resources," "The guidelines have not been given by our superiors," "There is a lack of personnel," "There are no incentives to work" — excuses which contrast the usual Cuban initiative, ingenuity and generally making do.

This initiative and ingenuity manifested itself in the 1993 anti-crime campaign in the capital, in the efforts to restore agriculture in the provinces razed by the so-called Storm of the Century and the unseasonal rains caused by the El Niño cyclone, as well as the efforts to use all available resources and seek imaginative and audacious solutions to problems.

If this problem is not resolved, the efforts made by many Cubans to overcome the effects of the blockade will be weakened, and the younger generation especially, who lack historical and economic experience but who can see the obvious deficiencies in the system, will draw their own conclusions. What is more, some argue that once the economic sanctions against Cuba have been lifted, President Fidel Castro will lose the justification for his rule and will be defeated.

In and out of Cuba, people have asked what would happen if we awoke one morning to news that the blockade had been lifted. Is the country prepared to face that kind of change? Experts agree that official U.S. thinking is frozen in the Cold War to justify their hegemony. They need an enemy to confront and humiliate, especially one like Cuba, with the force of its example and the success of its social model.

Beside, there is the weighty influence of a hardened sector of Cuban emigres, represented in Congress by the trio of Robert Menendez, Ileana Rose-Lethinen and Lincoln Díaz Balart, backed by the Cuban American National Foundation, Cuban Unity, Independent and Democratic Cuba and the paramilitary bands Alpha 66 and L. Commandos.

Nevertheless, the number of people with a different perspective on U.S.-Cuba relations is beginning to grow. On the Cuban American side, there is a broad range of organisations from liberals to centre right, such as Cuban Change, to others in the Cuban American Professional and Business Committee, the Cuban American Coalition and progressive groups, such as the Association of Cuban Workers, the Antonio Maceo Brigade and Casa de las Americas in New York, which have always been against the sanctions and have organised actions in solidarity and for humanitarian aid, even risking their lives and interests.

On the U.S. side there is a variety of views including traditional opponents of the blockade such as the John Hopkins academic Wayne Smith, former head of the U.S. Interests Section in Havana, and the delegation of the U.S. veterans of the Second World War, Vietnam, the Bay of Pigs and the Missile Crisis. In 1992, these veterans made a public declaration in Havana saying, "Cuba does not threaten the peace and security of the United States and the Cuban people suffer profoundly from the U.S. blockade. The Cuban conception of democracy is different from ours. Nevertheless, it is a right of nations to define their own political system in accordance with their cultural and historical traditions. That is why we call on the war veterans and the citizens of the United States to demand that Congress cancel the Torricelli Bill."

The president of the Political Commission of the U.S. Episcopal Conference, Archbishop John R. Roach, argues along similar lines, as does the religious leader and civil rights activist Reverend Jesse Jackson, when he called on his country to respect international law and self-determination and to normalize relations with Cuba. "It is certainly the time to put an end to the Cold War in this hemisphere and to allow freedom of trade and travel. . . The economic siege impedes the normal supply of petroleum, reduces Cuba's productive capacity, creates scarcity and revives the fear that the CIA will try to overthrow its government," affirmed Jackson in 1993.

More recently, the Reverend Jackson and his Rainbow Coalition have joined forces with the Interreligious Foundation for Community Work to coordinate efforts to confront the measures against Cuba. These efforts and others more recently have gained support from the major media for the first time. Articles and commentaries along these lines have appeared in the *Washington Post*, *New York Times*, *Wall Street Journal*, *Journal of Commerce* and the *World Trade* magazine.

U.S. VOTERS AND THE BLOCKADE

A *Time/CNN* opinion poll reported "that 64% of Americans are ready to talk with Castro, and a bare majority — 51% — thinks the embargo should not be lifted." *Time,* September 12, 1994

❖

A 1992 Tarrance Group poll indicated 67% of Americans thought Cuba posed no serious threat to U.S. security; 47% agreed that the United States should reestablish diplomatic and economic relations with Cuba; 65% opposed the United States imposing economic sanctions on other countries that trade or invest in Cuba; and 53% favored the lifting of the travel ban to Cuba.

❖

A poll released by the Commission on U.S. Latin American Relations in 1992 found that both Democratic and Republican voters are willing to see closer ties with Cuba: 58% support removing restrictions on mail and phone services to Cuba; 53% want an end to the U.S. travel ban; 46% support resuming economic ties with Cuba; and 47% support normal diplomatic relations.

❖

HISPANO-AMERICANS: Attitude to Cuba blockade

1994 poll of 4,800 Hispano-Americans in 10 U.S. cities by the Strategic Research Corporation found that 40% were against the maintenance of the embargo against Cuba (only 23% were in favor and 37% didn't know).
Results in Miami similarly indicated 40% against the embargo; with 36.4% in favor and 23.6% didn't know. (59% of those polled were Cuban Americans)

Dick Tobin, president of the Strategic Research Corporation concluded that the results showed the existence of a silent opposition to the blockade in Miami. Lisandro Pérez, director of the Institute of Cuba Investigations at the International University of Florida, said that the results confirmed a similar poll conducted by the *Miami Herald* in July 1993.

Source: *Miami Herald* February 2, 1994

Charles Rangel, a Democratic representative, is another person who has spoken in favor of lifting the sanctions and who promoted a bill (HR 2229) to restore free trade with Cuba. He called for complete freedom of trade, travel and communications. Rangel argued: "Democracy and human rights in Cuba would be better served if there could be a free flow of ideas and products instead of trying to isolate the country and thereby making ourselves responsible for the difficult lives of the poor Cuban people." His proposal now enjoyed the support of many members of Congress from both parties.

Former U.S. Attorney General Ramsey Clark has put forward a similar case, as did William Kunstler, the prominent U.S. constitutional lawyer, along with the Episcopal Conference and the Council of Churches of the United States. This point of view is even beginning to find a hearing in conservative sectors, among them Roger Fontaine, national security adviser to President Reagan; Ernest Preeg of the Center for Strategic and International Studies; and economist William Ratliff of the Hoover Institute.

For some, Cuba is a reminder of the Cold War. It is perhaps for that reason that the Administration is not able to admit, at least not publicly, the extent to which U.S. policy has become hostage to the vendettas of small national groupings.

While for many the problem of the blockade focuses on the disappearance of the figure of Fidel Castro, it is contradictory to maintain the blockade against Cuba, while lifting the sanctions against Vietnam, a socialist country with a single party, a state-run economy and party press, and with whom relations had been sadly affected by the memories of an inglorious war and thousands of dead.

Now, leaving all that aside, if the blockade were lifted, a potential export market of $1.3 billion to $2 billion would open to the U.S. businesses in the first year alone, according to recent studies carried out in the United States itself. They would immediately be able to sell Cuba $500 million of rice, $100 million of grain, $60 million in pharmaceuticals, and $95 million in chemicals.

The United States would also reduce its freight costs because it would be able to obtain all the nickel it needs for its industry only 90 miles from its coast, as well as citrus concentrates, rum, tobacco, fish, seafood and exclusive medicines that are the products of Cuban science. Furthermore, the resumption of trade with the Caribbean would directly benefit the local subsidiaries of U.S. firms and would favor the economies of the region.

According to the researcher Donna Rich Kaplowski of the John Hopkins University, successive U.S. administrations have caused as much damage to their own country as they have to the Cuban side. Business circles are now exerting pressure on the U.S. Department of Commerce not to continue losing opportunities. Many of them cautiously approach Cuban businesspeople or send exploratory missions to Cuba, as did Kentucky Fried Chicken in 1992. Companies, executives and banks throughout the world have turned their attention to the investment opportunities that are now offered in Cuba, and many U.S. businesses are irritated by their government's absurd behaviour.

So much so that in 1989 the trade attache of the Spanish embassy in Cuba, a fervent supporter of the investments by Spanish hotel chains in the tourist sector, remarked in a press interview that, "Sooner or later the U.S. embargo will be lifted, and when this happens these Spanish hotels are going to be ready to receive U.S. tourists."

For Cuba's part, Vice-President Carlos Lage commented, "All of our problems will not be resolved at once, but their solution will be greatly facilitated. Without producing one more ton of merchandise we would obtain hundreds of millions of additional dollars each year."

However, lifting the blockade would not mean the granting of generous terms of credit, with long-term payments or low interest rates; it would not mean large investments with quick returns because, even without the pressures of the blockade, we would have to negotiate with the same financial institutions that impose their rules worldwide; and creditors do not lend money if debts are not paid, or they demand economic measures that have a high social cost and that impinge on national independence.

Even in conditions of relative equality, Cuban products would have to compete fiercely for markets which are ruled by quotas, sometimes for fixed terms or quantities. Nor would there be access to the advanced technologies that are under the exclusive control of the developed nations. Until now, all the advantages of economic globalization have favored the industrial North, to the detriment of the underdeveloped South.

If the end of the blockade were decreed today, the largest of the Antilles would find itself at the threshold of an open door to a road without threats and full of opportunities, but without funds to buy anything, burdened with debts and still with numerous economic inefficiencies, combined with the need for structural, technological and business modernization — problems that would still be hard to overcome.

Everything might be easier, but the real challenge remains the same for the Cuban people: to work hard for the present and the future and not for what might happen if Washington changed its line. Without resources, current purchases must be limited to articles of basic necessity and any illusions can have damaging repercussions for the population.

"We see no sign that the U.S. blockade against Cuba will be lifted," Carlos Lage has stated. "I do not believe that the administration will change," said Cuban Foreign Minister Roberto Robaina. Meanwhile, President Clinton remarked, "I see no signs that [Cuba] — or the leadership, the government of President Castro — wants to make the kind of changes that we would expect before changing our policy."

One conflict, two positions and two concepts: the Cubans, who want to be themselves, for themselves, without depending on anyone. The United States, insisting that the Cubans cannot choose for themselves, but what the United States wants them to be.

Despite all that has happened, despite all the world forums where the blockade has been condemned as illegal, unjust, immoral, in violation of the Universal Declaration of Human Rights, and even irrational and against the interests of the United States, the blockade continues, unsuccessful in its attempt to overthrow the Cuban socialist project and bring about a change of government. Cuba's very existence and its tenacious resistance are a monument to the failure of this aggressive policy.

This is the Caribbean Wall that many try not to see, the Iron Curtain that survives the Cold War, a wall used to try to isolate Cuba and disguise the fact that despite all predictions, Cuba continues to resist and develop.

IF THE BLOCKADE WERE LIFTED...

- the U.S. could export up to $400 million in grain sales to Cuba
- the U.S. could supply all Cuba's fertilizer and pesticide requirements (totalling around $150 million)
- U.S. agricultural sales to Cuba could be an estimated $300 million
- Cuba would purchase about $90 million in U.S. medical supplies
- the U.S. could sell Cuba 20,000 tons of cotton, 5,000 polyester and rayon fibers and about $1 million of thread
- U.S. port authorities anticipate a dramatic expansion in shipping
- by purchasing Cuban citrus, the U.S. could save $34 million a year
- U.S. could capture 60% of Cuba's nickel exports
- $6.5 million per year could be saved by purchasing Cuban sugar
- cheaper U.S. imports of Cuban seafood, coffee, tobacco, rum, honey and marble
- U.S. tourist industry and cruise lines could benefit around $1 billion a year

TRADE OPPORTUNITIES

In 1992, the John Hopkins University published a report* estimating that if normal commercial relations were restored, the total trade turnover between the United States and Cuba could be $6.5 billion a year within a few years. Cuba currently imports $4 billion worth of goods.

MEANWHILE

- Mexican and Italian firms have signed billion dollar joint ventures to improve Cuba's international telephone system
- European, Canadian and Latin American firms explore for oil off Cuba's coasts
- Spanish and Canadian hotel chains are investing in major tourist developments
- Israel is engaged in a joint venture with Cuba for citrus production and marketing

*Source: "New opportunities for U.S.- Cuban trade" by Donna Rich Kaplowitz & Michael Kaplowitz (April 1992) John Hopkins University

Impact of the blockade
by Roberto Robaina
Cuban Foreign Minister

◆

In a letter dated June 25, 1993, to the UN Secretary-General, Cuban Foreign Minister Robaina reviewed the impact of the blockade:

I have the honor of addressing myself to you, on behalf of the government of the Republic of Cuba, regarding your Note of 14 April, 1993, through which you requested all pertinent information on compliance with Resolution 47/19 of the UN General Assembly, entitled "On the need to put an end to the economic, commercial and financial embargo of Cuba imposed by the United States." The government and the people of Cuba are confident in the United Nations' ability and commitment to eradicating a situation which indisputably is in violation of international law and of the recognized norms and principles governing relations among nations.

Compliance with Resolution 47/19 of the General Assembly would imply that the United States, as part of the international community and, in particular, as a member state of the United Nations, refrain from "promulgating and applying laws and measures. . . whose extraterritorial effects affect the sovereignty of other states and the legitimate interests of entities or persons under their jurisdiction, and the freedom of trade and navigation." It would also imply that the United States take "the necessary steps" to eliminate or annul the effects of laws or measures of that nature, which exist and are applied as part and parcel of the hostile policy followed by that country against Cuba.

Facts, on the other hand, point in the opposite direction. The United States, by continuing and intensifying their policy of economic blockade against Cuba, is in violation of this resolution, as well as the principles of "sovereign equality of States, non-intervention and non-interference in their internal affairs, freedom of trade and international navigation," reaffirmed in its Preamble.

The broad and profound debate that took place in the General Assembly on November 24, 1992, and Resolution 47/19 there adopted, confirmed the illegal and unjust nature of the economic, commercial and financial blockade imposed by the U.S. government against Cuba, and should at least have led to a reconsideration of that absurd policy of aggression, which violates not only the most basic human rights of the Cuban people, but also the sovereign rights of third countries.

Moreover, in clear defiance of the will of the international community, the U.S. government has geared its actions to reinforcing the blockade with measures of a legal and regulatory character, as well as with undercover and defamation acts, including exerting pressure and blackmail against others. All this is within the context of a hostile network of sanctions built and applied with the overt aim of overthrowing the political and economic system existing in Cuba and replacing it by another more to the liking of the United States.

With the application of this policy, the U.S. government is not only in violation of Resolution 47/19 of the General Assembly, but also directly violates Resolutions 38/197, 39/210, 40/185, 41/165, 42/173, 44/215 and 46/210 of that body, all of which deplore the adoption of economic measures aimed at exercising coercion against sovereign decisions taken by developing countries. Furthermore, it ignores the expressed will of the Heads of State or Government of the Movement of Nonaligned Countries, who in their 10th Summit Conference urged "the U.S. government to cease its unfriendly acts against Cuba and to terminate the series of economic, commercial and financial measures and actions imposed upon that country for over three decades, which have inflicted enormous material losses and economic damage." On that occasion, the Heads of State or Government "further called upon the United States to resolve its differences with Cuba through negotiations on the basis of equality and mutual respect."

Extraterritorial nature of U.S. blockade

The very wide scope of legal regulatory actions and practices carried out by the United States with the objective of economically strangling Cuba, since its inception has had an extraterritorial nature affecting not only Cuba, but also third countries and the normal flow of international economic relations. This was the case even before the so-called Torricelli law [Cuban Democracy Act], which reinforced the blockade, and expressly formalized a *de facto* situation, reiterating extraterritorial measures that the United States had applied against Cuba in the 1960s.

The U.S. government is in violation of Resolution 47/19, first and foremost, because its economic aggression against Cuba is based precisely on Federal and State laws and regulations, consciously promulgated against international law, and pursuing clear aims of economic coercion. The very existence of those laws and regulations affects the sovereignty of Cuba as an independent state and constitutes an attempt at intervening and interfering in its internal affairs. It equally affects the sovereignty of third countries and the freedom of trade and international navigation, enshrined in numerous international legal instruments to which the United States is party. Since the adoption of Resolution 47/19 by the General Assembly, the U.S. government has not taken a single step, from the legal and regulatory point of view, toward rectifying this policy which it maintains in complete defiance of the principles contained in the Charter of the United Nations and the norms governing international relations.

In addition, after the approval of Resolution 47/19 of the General Assembly, the Congress of the United States has been examining new legislative instruments that accentuate the extraterritorial nature of the blockade by tying the eligibility of any foreign government to receive economic assistance from the United States, to the nature of its commercial relations with Cuba. Clauses in the Foreign Assistance Authorization Act of 1993 adopted on June 16, 1993, by the House of Representatives are an example of the above.

Instead of refraining from promulgating and applying new "laws and measures" and of taking "the necessary steps" to eliminate or annul the effects of those already in place as called for by Resolution 47/19, the U.S. government allows and promotes in the States comprising the Union, the passage of laws which are — if it were possible — even more in violation of international law, aimed at dictating limits to sovereign states or nationals of those states in their economic relations with Cuba.

Such is the case of the law promulgated on May 20, 1993, in the State of Florida, which includes legal and economic reprisals against those corporations that carry out trade or maintain economic links with Cuba and either have headquarters or interests in the State of Florida, irrespective of their private or governmental character.

This new law no longer only affects the sovereignty of other states by attempting to restrict the activities of U.S. subsidiaries in third countries, actions condemned by the international community, but also limits the rights of persons, entities and governments which in no way fall within the jurisdiction of the United States.

The intensity and range of the actions described below demonstrate all the characteristics of an aggression through economic means. By creating economic difficulties for Cuba affecting the health, wellbeing, peace and standard of living of the population, these actions have the declared aim of overthrowing the political, economic and social system that the Cuban people have freely chosen. It is the task of the United Nations to consider and deal with thse actions in conformity with the responsibilities conferred upon it by the Principles and Purpose of the organization as enshrined in the Charter.

The U.S. government has been exercising direct pressure upon governments in our region to hinder the establishment and development of commmercial relations with Cuba and to prevent Cuba from adhering to regional integration and coordination organizations in particular sectors, such as tourism. Specifically, during 1992, the U.S. government directed threats to several of those governments warning them of the "cost" of their commercial and economic relations with Cuba.

Through official channels, the U.S. government has addressed itself to a number of governments with which Cuba has been negotiating barter agreements for the exchange of sugar, oil, nickel and other products with the purpose of blocking these deals. Three countries in Latin America were the target of intimidation by the U.S. government. In one case, pressures were not only directed to trade in oil, but even to agreements regarding technical assistance by that country to the Cuban oil industry.

The United States used the stipulations of the so-called Torricelli law, even before it was put into effect, to intimidate the above-mentioned governments, invoking the discretionary authority conferred by the law to the President of the United States to impose sanctions upon any country that provides assistance to Cuba.

An important member state of the European Community has been receiving strong pressure from the United States to withdraw its credits to Cuba, and has even been threatened with the adoption of measures, in GATT, against its interests. In the context of "diplomatic" actions, the U.S. officials have openly acknowledged that their country's policy is to pressure other countries and prevent further success by Cuba in its efforts to expand its commercial base. To that end they have used the tactics of creating the false fear that any commercial operation with Cuba entails high risks.

Pressure on oil producers

During 1992, the U.S. government itself embarked on the systematic search for information on possible oil sales to Cuba and potential vendors. To that end, the United States launched an offensive through their embassies in oil-producing countries in the Caribbean, Latin America, Africa, Asia and the Middle East, so as to prevent oil sales to Cuba. Some of those countries were explicitly warned that any sale to Cuba could negatively influence their relations with the United States, and could create difficulties in the granting of credits by institutions such as the International Monetary Fund or the World Bank.

In the case of African countries, the message was even more explicit, warning them that restrictions by the World Bank or the IMF could affect the granting of resources for drought relief programs.

These pressures have also been, directly or indirectly, exerted on several foreign companies negotiating with Cuba regarding oil exploration in the Cuban continental shelf. Such is the case of the French company **Total**, whose offices in Paris were visited by emissaries of the U.S. government alleging that the area offered by Cuba for prospecting and exploitation had legally registered owners from before 1959.

With the same objectives, the United States has used consulting firms and scientific bodies, both within the U.S. and abroad, to publish fake studies aimed at providing disinformation on the real prospects for Cuban oil. The oil firm **Petroconsult** of the University of Houston, Texas, is one of the institutions used for this purpose.

The United States also began a rumor campaign in the international media about the possible withdrawal from Cuba of some of these companies, such as **Total**, with the aim of creating doubts and uncertainty regarding the real possibilities for oil exploration in Cuba.

At least one Latin American government and one European government received visits from U.S. officials who conveyed Washington's grave concern with respect to any type of cooperation with Cuba in oil joint ventures. In other cases in Latin America, the U.S. government in late 1992 informed top government spheres of those countries that by virtue of the Torricelli law, provision of fuel to Cuban commercial planes should be suspended.

Access to sugar markets denied

Another key action by the U.S. government in applying the blockade has been to procure alternate sources of sugar to state members of the

Commonweath of Independent States, with the objective of displacing Cuban exports from their markets and thus depriving Cuba from export income.

During 1992, the United States assisted some of those republics in identifying possible alternate sources of sugar and persuaded them not to conclude barter agreements of oil for sugar with other countries interested in similar barter agreements and mediated between those potential suppliers and the CIS.

On the other hand, the United States called upon a number of governments in Latin America and the Caribbean to participate in sugar barter operations with the CIS, even knowing that such agreements are contrary to the interests of those countries, as they go against privatization programs that the United States itself is trying to impose in the region. Furthermore, the CIS cannot constitute a viable market for those Latin American and Caribbean countries on account of long distances and their lack of convertible currency.

The ex-Assistant Secretary of State for Inter-American Affairs, Bernard Aronson, undertook personal steps in Washington to that end, clearly demonstrating the priority that the U.S. government attached to this issue. Aronson himself requested William Middendorf, ex-Ambassador of the United States to the Organization of American States and now chair of a consulting firm dealing with investment and trade projects in Latin America, to gather the necessary information regarding possible suppliers for the government of an important trade partner of Cuba in the region.

By mid-1992, that country's Ministry of Foreign Affairs had obtained a list of possible suppliers, obviously provided by the United States, among which were several countries and private enterprises.

During all of 1992, efforts to neutralize new agreements that would involve special credits to Cuba to facilitate the purchase of medicines, or the Cuban sale of pharmaceutical and biotechnological products, were continued as part of the U.S. policy of harassment against Cuba. These actions were particularly harsh in Latin America. The U.S. government pressured several Latin American governments with the aim of blocking Cuba's sale of medical products to these countries. It also attempted to prevent the purchase by Cuba of medical products which are lacking, such as plasma, hormones for the thyroid gland, penicillin, antibiotics, alkaloids and cortisone.

This situation has not changed during 1993. Restrictions preventing the sale of medical products by U.S. companies to Cuba are still in place. By the same token, any company, anywhere in the world, is forbidden from selling to Cuba any medicine, medical equipment or medical supply which contains components or parts, or technologies of U.S. origin. This has had particularly adverse effects for Cuba, as it is aggravates shortages which seriously affect the country's health care programs at this time.

The U.S. government continues to put pressure on companies in third countries to sever their economic links to Cuba, invoking restrictions imposed by the blockade and, more recently, by the Torricelli law.

The following are examples of these pressures:

- The United States pressured the British sugar company **Tate and Lyle** to sever its economic links with Cuba after company representatives participated in a sugar forum held in Cuba in May 1992.
- The British communications company, **Cable and Wireless**, a subsidiary of which is located in U.S. territory, was threatened by the U.S. government that any investment in Cuba would result in the rejection of the licence it had requested to operate between Europe and Asia through the United States.
- In November 1992, the Mexican newspaper *El Financiero* revealed that the owners of the **María Isabel Sheraton** hotel in Mexico had been the object of strong pressure by the U.S. Embassy and that such pressure had caused the cancellation of a Cuban contract.
- That same Mexican newspaper also revealed the pressures personally applied by the U.S. Ambassador, John D. Negroponte, on the **Monterrey Group** to prevent, in this case, the creation of a joint venture with Cuba in the textile industry.
- The U.S. government has created obstacles to Cuba's purchase of respiratory valves, connectors, pressure boxes, nebulizers, micro-nebulizer flasks, etc., all of them spare parts for the **Bird** respirator, most widely used in intensive and intermediate care units, post-surgical wards and asthmatics wards in Cuban hospitals, as well as in emergency services.
- Executives of the Canadian medical company **Eli Lilly Canada Inc.** recently stated that as a result of U.S. laws, in particular the Torricelli law, the sale of their products to Cuba was forbidden. One of those executives explained that because **Eli Lilly Canada Inc.** is a subsidiary of the U.S. company **Eli Lilly and Co.** (the world's leading insulin producer), they were forbidden to trade with Cuba or Cuban companies, even if their exports included medicines

for common diseases such as vascular disorders, lung disease, cancer, etc.
- In October 1992, the Argentine newspaper *Pagina 12* revealed that the two main cereal companies operating in Argentina, **Cargill SACI** and **Compania Continental CACINF**, had decided to suspend their grain exports to Cuba as a result of the Torricelli law. According to forecasts, those exports would have amounted to $100 million through the sale of only wheat, soy beans, green peas and lentils. Such a decision by **Cargill** and **Continental** was contrary to these companies' interests, and even their executives admitted that the decision taken was highly damaging. Executives of **Continental Grain**, which has a main office (**Continental CACINF**) in the United States, privately admitted that they had been visited by U.S. government officials, who warned them that if they did not stop trade with Cuba, their company would be seriously affected.

Pressures by the United States to reinforce the blockade have also been put on the shipping sector, with the aim of further limiting Cuba's opportunities for foreign trade which are vital in the current conditions for the development of Cuba's economy.

Sources close to European shipping organizations verify that immediately after the statement [in April 1992] by the ex-President of the United States, George Bush, closing U.S. ports to ships transporting merchandise or passengers to or from Cuba, the U.S. government informed European and Latin American shipping companies that the U.S. authorities would impound or impose high fines on vessels violating this law.

The following are more examples of cases involving U.S. pressure on third countries:
- A statement of intention for the shipping of 25,000 tons of wheat was withdrawn on account of problems faced by the exporter to obtain a freight quote to Cuba by Latin American shipping companies.
- Other wheat exports by European companies have been frustrated on account of difficulties of sending vessels to Cuba.
- A major Asian company that was a traditional carrier of Cuban imports was compelled to sever its contract with Cuba, as its ships in the Caribbean must necessarily enter U.S. Pacific ports.
- By virtue of the blockade laws, the U.S. Treasury Department recently arrogated upon itself the right to freeze a bank

transfer from a Latin American bank, through the Atlantic Bank in the United States, to the Havana International Bank in London. The operation was for the payment of a credit granted by the "Empresa de Navegación Mambisa" of Cuba to cover transportation costs of agricultural equipment.

During 1993 this has been aggravated because of the refusal of shipping companies to trade with Cuba as a result of strong pressures brought to bear upon them, thus creating seriously difficulties for the transport of basic foodstuffs for the Cuban people.

The field of tourism has also been targeted by the U.S. government. According to dispatches from the AFP press agency and *The Toronto Star*, Canadian travel agencies cannot make reservations to and from Cuba, not even via third countries. This is because the U.S. firm whose data base feeds the reservations computer system used by Canadian companies decided on June 20, 1993, to refuse such service and thus compelled Canadian companies to join the blockade, without it being either in their interest or their intention.

The aggressive attitude by the United States has reached such extremes as to obstruct donations of a humanitarian nature to Cuba. The difficulties faced by the movement "Va por Cuba" in Mexico to send an oil tanker to Cuba were a consequence of those pressures. Officials of the U.S. Embassy in Mexico personally devoted themselves to pressuring officials of PEMEX to prevent the dispatch of the tanker.

The United States has also attempted to prevent Cuba from receiving other donations, such as that offered by the Italian entity **Enel Spa**, valued at $4 million, for the "Union Electrica" of the Cuban Ministry of Basic Industry. While preparing the donation, **Enel Spa** received a note suggesting that they should take into account their close commercial and financial links with the United States, and they were warned of the negative consequences the donation could entail in conformity with the Torricelli law.

There is a number of means, Secretary-General, to measure the effects of this aggression against Cuba, both from the economic as well as from the social point of view, and many experts in a number of fields have generated sufficient documentation about this. A profound and conscientious study by the United Nations is still lacking. To do so is totally within its responsibilities, and Cuba is ready to provide as much information as necessary to that end. The inescapable conclusion is that the U.S. aim of inflicting suffering upon the Cuban people does not yet reach unbearable proportions only because of the just and equitable social policy that characterizes the Cuban revolutionary process and ensures national unity and the will of Cubans to resist. Nevertheless, the economic and social effects are enormous and unquestionably constitute a flagrant and massive violation of the human rights of the Cuban people.

Cost to Cuba

According to some estimates, the blockade has cost Cuba more than $40 billion, which is the approximate equivalent of twenty times the country's current account revenue for 1992. Its effects have been present in practically all sectors of the economy, and have had an accumulative effect over more than 30 years, bringing about changes in the consumption patterns of the population, huge investments in the industrial and transportation sectors, among others, that otherwise would not have been necessary, and difficulties for scientific and technical development, as well as significant shortages in certain consumer goods for the population at large.

Cuba purchases imports at higher prices because of the blockade, the sources of these goods are limited and Cuba is billed for the risk assumed by the seller when trading with an enemy of the United States. By the same token, our country has to sell cheap. All this results from economic relations that are subjected to the vagrancies of an economic warfare waged against Cuba by the strongest economic, technological and military power in the world.

As a consequence of pressures and obstacles imposed by the blockade, Cuba has to seek imports from extremely distant markets, increasing the price of transportation. It is also compelled to maintain large inventories in warehouses and cold storage plants, with the resulting rise in costs.

The restrictions on free shipping of those merchant vessels involved in trade with Cuba has brought about, among other things, delays in the acquisition of imports, determining lack of supplies of additional consumer goods; even greater difficulties in maintaining national health care programs; and the idling of industrial plants producing either consumer goods for the population or export products.

For example, in 1992, and considering only grains, chicken and milk as basic foodstuffs for the population, Cuba paid an excess of US$41.5 on account of price differences. It lost more than $85 million on freight alone; Cuba's freight costs for fuel were 43 percent more expensive, and this increased three-fold for other products. Equally, during the first four months of 1993, the import of grains, wheat and edible oil alone cost the country an estimated $1,329,876 above the market freight value.

The illegitimate freezing of Cuban telecommunications assets in the United States amounts to more than $102 million and, considering the principal plus interest, increases by $7 million annually.

As a result of economic pressure and additional problems in the international sugar market — the main source of income for Cuba — the country has been compelled to sell all its sugar exports in the residual market, where the price is approximately 50 percent of what it reaches in the so-called principal markets. Even so, being prevented from pricing its sugar in the New York Stock Exchange as a consequence of the blockade Cuba has to concede a discount to its clients, even below the prices of the residual market. This amounts to an added reduction in income of $30 million.

Furthermore, Cuba has suffered enormous losses by not being able to carry out economic transactions in U.S. dollars. Blockade regulations forbid banks in third countries from maintaining accounts in dollars for Cuba and Cuban nationals, and also the use of this currency or of accounts in U.S. dollars for transactions between nationals of third countries and Cuban nationals. It is obvious that, considering the weight of the U.S. dollar in the international economy, the losses due to monetary transfers and rates of exchange are substantial.

This situation has been made even worse during the last months of 1992 and early 1993 when the impact of the so-called Torricelli law has been increasingly felt. The formal legalization of the extraterritorial reach of the blockade has had a negative impact upon numerous transactions that were being carried out until recently, in spite of existing difficulties.

The implications of this situation demonstrate the inhumanity of those who have started and waged this type of war against Cuba. It has been amply proven by the fact that, since the start, foodstuffs and medicines have been included within the scope of U.S. manufactured products or containing elements of U.S. origin, to which access is forbidden to the Cuban people. It can also be proven that Cuba's trade with subsidiaries of United States companies abroad, which have been targeted by the 1992 Torricelli law, primarily involves the purchase of foodstuffs and medicines essential to cover basic consumption needs of the Cuban people.

In that regard, the official information published annually by the U.S. Treasury Department in the document entitled "Special Report:

Analysis of Licenced Trade with Cuba by Foreign Subsidiaries of United States Companies" is a useful reference.

Consequently, foodstuffs and primary products for manufacture in Cuba have to be purchased in distant markets and subjected to problems of additional costs, freights, bonuses, etc., which hinder all of Cuba's commercial activity.

A recent example of this related to the imports needed in the struggle to eradicate the disease known as the neuropathy epidemic, which received widespread publicity. For a partial shipment alone of a contract for vitamins and excipients for the manufacture of the tablets that, as a preventative measure, were being provided to those affected and to the population at large, the country was compelled to spend some US$237,448 for air freight from Europe. If the blockade measures hadn't prevented access to the U.S. market for purchasing these products, such expenditure could have been reduced by US$181,548.

It is important to emphasize that the direct effect of the blockade on the Cuban population is not greater thanks to the just and equitable way in which the country's resources are distributed, and to 33 years of conscious and dedicated investment in the social sector, aimed at increasing the standard of living, nutrition, health, education and dignity of the Cuban people. But this fact does not absolve the U.S. government from its responsibility for committing one of the most prolonged and flagrant crimes in recent history, and does not absolve it from its obligations in the face of the demands of the international community in conformity with Resolution 47/19 of the General Assembly, the principles governing the United Nations and international law.

We are certain, Excellency, that your dedication to this issue and the content of the report you will present, will provide this organization an opportunity to play an active role in putting an end to a situation, as unjust as it is anachronistic. This would be a further occasion to renew your commitment to peace and cooperation before the United Nations and the international community.

On behalf of the Cuban government, allow me to reiterate once more our readiness to work with you in every aspect that would contribute to promote cooperation to ensure the balanced development of international relations and a dignified life for all peoples, in conformity with the Charter.

Receive, Excellency, the assurances of my most distinguished consideration.

❖❖❖

The U.S. blockade of Cuba

In a letter of July 22, 1994, Cuban Foreign Minister Roberto Robaina again reviewed progress toward the implementation of UN resolutions 47/19 and 48/16 condemning the U.S. blockade of Cuba. He concluded that far from complying with these resolutions and refraining from pressuring other countries to apply the blockade, "the United States has reinforced the blockade with legal, covert, intimidatory and defamatory measures, including blackmail, against third countries."

"In practical terms," he writes, "Resolution 48/16 is unfulfilled by the continuation and the reinforcement of measures aimed at preventing and hindering Cuba's economic links with the world.

"Some countries have introduced various provisions in their national legislation to avoid the extraterritorial implementation of. . . the Torricelli Act. . . . Nonetheless, in 1993, the commercial trade with Cuba of U.S. subsidiaries in third countries virtually disappeared as a result of the application of this Act."

Robaina describes how the prohibited entry into U.S. ports for 180 days of vessels transporting cargo or passengers to and from Cuba, which in effect is a six month ban, has cost Cuba an additional $34 million for food imports, and increased oil freight costs by 15 to 30 percent. "In general, the economic losses because of this situation, last year amounted to more than $50 million.

"For example, $398,588 more was paid to transport medicines from Europe, which could have purchased 5.6 tons of Chloranfenicol, a broad-spectrum antibiotic. . . .

"The new measures applied against Cuba make the already existing difficulties more acute due to the loss of external private sources of finance. The U.S. pressures and actions on financial institutions prevent them from providing any type of aid to Cuba or put priority on extending credits.

"Although it has tried to use more subtle methods. . . the U.S. government has not refrained from using official channels to pressure any country that provides economic assistance to Cuba."

Robaina goes on to mention several examples of U.S. attempts to spoil Cuban business deals concerning oil, sugar, and even a UN supervised energy program. Washington, he says, has also recently exerted pressure on the emerging Association of Caribbean States, the Ibero-American summit and a meeting of African foreign ministers to isolate Cuba. "Russian-Cuban economic and commercial relations have been under continuous harassment from the U.S. government, which has used various methods to disrupt joint business ventures."

"During this period, U.S. pressures were also exerted on several foreign enterprises that had already decided or are negotiating to invest in the exploration and prospecting for Cuban oil. . . .

"The State Department made contact with several U.S. oil companies whose properties were nationalized. . . the purpose being to 'warn' each company that the growing foreign investment in Cuba could complicate their property claims and create serious political and legal problems."

"One of the U.S. government's priorities," he continues, "has been to identify foreign partners of Cuban enterprises in order to neutralize them." In this regard, Robaina lists businesses in Honduras, Columbia, Britain, Holland, Germany, Canada, Sweden and Australia whose dealings with Cuba were discouraged, disrupted or blocked by U.S. interference in recent years. These include:

- In March 1994, the U.S. ambassador to Britain personally approached a prominent British businessman to discourage his planned trip to Cuba
- A German business executive considering investment in Cuba was similarly pressured
- The Canadian enterprise **Sherrit Gordon** was dissuaded from establishing a joint venture with Cuba
- Australian company **Teratonics** was forbidden to sell their heart pacemakers to Cuba because their product had U.S. components
- Within days of a U.S. company takeover, **Siemens Elemac** of Sweden was forced to cancel a sale of pacemakers to Cuba
- The Bacardi company addressed a letter to the Association of Rum Producers of the West Indies warning that they intend to make legal claim to their property in Cuba and seek compensation
- Conscious efforts have been made to divert tourist trade from Cuba to Puerto Rico
- A Central American tourist company received threats from a high-ranking U.S. embassy official to cease operations in Cuba because they were allegedly in violation of the Torricelli law

Robaina concludes: "It is evident that the efforts of the U.S. government to tighten the blockade are aimed at preventing the Cuban people's access to essential products and services such as energy, medicines, foodstuffs and other basic goods that directly affect the quality of life. These efforts are also aimed at hindering the capacity of the Cuban economy to produce these goods and generate the hard currency resources needed for their purchase."

The United States government stands alone, defying the will of the nations of the world, in its commission of this crime against humanity. It acts in the interest of a handful of economic groups which want to steal the assets of Cuba for their own profit and impoverish the Cuban people whose revolution brought health, freedom from want and universal education shared with the poor throughout the planet. Stop this outrage.

Ramsey Clark
(former U.S. attorney general)

❖

The embargo is counterproductive and wrong from a humanistic, a legal, a political and an economic point of view. It is the quintessence of failed foreign policy. According to a poll published last month by the *Miami Herald*, only a minority of the Cuban American community in Miami supports the embargo policy.

Andrew Zimbalist
(Professor of Economics at Smith College)

❖

From this materially bloated, spiritually impoverished country, where so many are homeless and starving, I've admired Cuba's struggle to share its meager resources so that all might stand proud. People around the world admire the Cuban people because they have exhibited an incredible love, active and sacrificing, for all — humans and planet — that is oppressed, all that suffers. Now, as Cuba suffers, we are called upon to act.

Alice Walker

Questions and answers about the blockade

✧

[The following interview with Michael Krinsky is excerpted from *CUBA Update* Summer 1994. Krinsky is a member of the New York law firm Rabinowitz, Boudin, Standard, Krinsky & Luberman, which represents the government of Cuba and its agencies in the United States.]

How was the embargo imposed in the first place?
The U.S. embargo against Cuba is as comprehensive as any the United States has ever mounted. It is modelled on the World War II embargo against the Axis powers. In early 1961, the State Department was considering an actual naval blockade of the island to cut off Cuba's commerce with the world. The Treasury Department advised the State Department that it could accomplish almost the same result by imposing the economic embargo in place today under the Trading With the Enemy Act.

What effect does the embargo have on U.S. citizens?
With very limited exceptions, the U.S. embargo prohibits persons subject to United States jurisdiction from engaging in any transaction which may benefit Cuba or Cuban nationals. So, we cannot buy from the Cubans, sell to the Cubans, hire Cubans, be employed by Cubans, make gifts to Cubans or even donate services to Cubans.

Why do you think the embargo and the politics surrounding it have lasted so long?
This is well beyond my expertise, but perhaps I can offer a few useful observations.

Presidential ambitions and Florida's electoral vote seem now, as they have in the past, to be critical. But, now as before, there seems to be a deeper way in which Washington and Miami's perception of their interests coincide to perpetuate and reinforce the embargo.

When the Bush Administration was asked why it maintained the embargo against Cuba but favored trade on a most favored nation basis with China, it answered that China was moving towards a market economy but Cuba was not. Secretary of State Christopher gave the same answer when he first assumed office and has since coined the phrase "market democracy" to encapsulate the Administration's goal in Cuba and elsewhere. The Cuban Democracy Act expresses the same policy by prescribing Cuba's adoption of a market economy as one of the conditions which will trigger a "Presidential Obligation" to lift the embargo.

President Bush went to Miami to sign the Cuban Democracy Act and there, surrounded by Jorge Mas Canosa and the rest of the Miami crowd, expressed to their delight that he would not rest until the treasured liberty of economic opportunity as well as freedom of speech and religion were restored in Cuba.

We do not know whether, without the political pressure from Miami, the Clinton Administration would maintain the embargo until Cuba agrees to become Warren Christopher's "market democracy." There are other, more subtle views of U.S. interests in Cuba and how they might be obtained. If the exile community fragments in Miami, perhaps we will find out.

Is it true that the embargo is stricter now than it used to be?
Yes. The Cuban Democracy Act of 1992 withdrew two important concessions the U.S. made to its allies in the mid-1970s who were eager to trade with Cuba without Washington's interference. First and most importantly perhaps, the Cuban Democracy Act revived the "blacklist" of third country vessels that trade in Cuban ports. Under the CDA, the U.S. bars any third country vessel from loading or unloading cargo in U.S. ports for 180 days after trading in goods or passengers on board bound to or from Cuba. Second, the CDA makes the embargo applicable to third country companies owned by U.S. nationals to the same extent as U.S. companies.

President Clinton implemented the Cuban Democracy Act, which he had endorsed as a candidate. While there were some opportunities to soften the CDA's impact through interpretation and licensing policies, the Clinton Administration has not followed that course. The Clinton Administration has also been vigorous in its enforcement of the embargo in other respects. Most telling, it has not moved to relax the travel ban even though there is clear support in Congress for such a move — now formalized in a "Sense of the Congress" resolution opposing restrictions on educational and similar travel. To the same effect, the Administration has refused to let U.S. companies implement freely negotiated telephone agreements with Cuba even though there is a strong demand in the Cuban American community for normal telephone service and Congress has provided ample political cover in the CDA.

Can U.S. citizens travel to Cuba at all? Would we automatically be able to travel freely to Cuba if the embargo were lifted?
The embargo's sweeping prohibitions prevent most of us from traveling to Cuba. Under the embargo, we cannot pay for lodging or meals and so we cannot visit the island unless we are fully hosted.

There are quite limited exceptions to the embargo's prohibitions. By far the most important are the special accommodations Washington grants to the Cuban American community, whose members insist on visiting and helping their families in Cuba. Cuban Americans are permitted to pay up to $100 per day in travel expenses in order to visit their close relatives on the island. They are permitted to send up to $300 every three months to each close relative on the island. They, as well as others, are permitted to send gift parcels valued at $200 per month to each donee. The resulting flow of hard currency to the island is substantial.*

Family visits account for most of the travel to Cuba and there is a brisk business for the U.S. air charterers which are licenced to carry this and other lawful travel between Miami and Havana. There are additionally exceptions for professionals pursuing research of an academic nature about Cuba, and news gatherers. Few U.S. citizens can qualify under these exceptions, whether they want to go to Cuba to learn about a different society or to visit the beaches.

If the embargo were lifted, all United States citizens could travel freely to Cuba. The current restrictions are on the payment of expenses necessary for travel, not on the travel itself. It is worth noting that the President could lift the restrictions on travel without otherwise relaxing the embargo. So too could Congress.

---

*New measures were imposed in August 1994 by the Clinton Administration which restricted the transfer of currency from the United States to Cuba; cut back on charter flights between the two countries; and further limited the ability of U.S. citizens to travel to Cuba.

As the lawyer handling many negotiations with Cuba, can you tell us which industries or businesses have shown the most interest in dealing with Cuba?
U.S. business is interested in almost every possible form of trade and investment with Cuba. It is not happy to see competitors from Canada, Spain, France, Italy, Germany, Mexico and elsewhere forming joint ventures and pursuing other business opportunities in every sector of the Cuban economy. U.S. business is increasingly tired and skeptical of the Administration's position that it need only hold on a little longer and the Castro government will fall, leaving a clear path to reenter Cuba. For the first time there are now visible efforts by large U.S. companies to assert their interests with the Administration.

The embargo's prohibitions extend equally to dealings with the Cuban government and individual Cuban nationals. They extend as well to transactions with third country nationals which may indirectly benefit Cuba. For example, we cannot buy a third country's product containing materials of Cuban origin. By this and other extraterritorial extensions of the embargo to third countries, the U.S. seeks to isolate Cuba from the world economy.

What would be immediately different if the embargo were lifted?
If the embargo were lifted, trade and other financial transactions as well as travel between the two countries could be resumed. However, commercial and financial relations would not necessarily be normal. Cuba would not have "most favored nation" status, so most of its goods would be subject to quite high tariffs. Likewise, foreign aid and other forms of assistance meant to facilitate trade and investment still would not be available. U.S. representatives to international lending institutions still would be under instructions to block assistance to Cuba. In other words, the U.S. would still have a great deal of economic leverage and presumably would exercise it in the same fashion as it is doing, or trying, with respect to China and other countries.

APPENDICES

Appendix 1

KENNEDY, CUBA AND CIGARS

By Pierre Salinger
[Excerpted from *Cigar Aficionado*, Vol. 1, No. 1, Autumn 1992]

Shortly after I entered the White House in 1961, a series of dramatic events occurred. In April 1961, the United States went through the disastrous error of the Bay of Pigs where Cuban exiles with the help of the United States government tried to overthrow the government of Fidel Castro. Several months later, the President called me into his office early in the evening.

"Pierre, I need some help," he said solemnly.

"I'll be glad to do anything I can Mr. President," I replied.

"I need a lot of [Cuban] cigars."

"How many, Mr. President?"

"About 1,000 Petit Upmanns."

I shuddered a bit, although I kept my reaction to myself. "And when do you need them, Mr. President?"

"Tomorrow morning."

I walked out of the office wondering if I would succeed. But since I was now a solid Cuban cigar smoker, I knew a lot of stores, and I worked on the problem into the evening.

The next morning, I walked into my White House office at about 8 a.m., and the direct line from the President's office was already ringing. He asked me to come in immediately.

"How did you do Pierre?" he asked, as I walked through the door.

"Very well," I answered. In fact, I'd gotten 1,200 cigars. Kennedy smiled, and opened up his desk. He took out a long paper which he immediately signed. It was the decree banning all Cuban products from the United States. Cuban cigars were now illegal in our country. . . .

Appendix 2

RESOLUTION 47/19 Approved by the United Nations General Assembly, November 24, 1992

"On the need to put an end to the economic, commercial and financial embargo against Cuba imposed by the United States"

The General Assembly, determined to encourage strict compliance with the purposes and principles recognized by the Charter of the United Nations, stressing, among other principles, the sovereign equality of nations, non-intervention and non-interference in their internal affairs, the freedom of international trade and navigation, also recognized in other international legal documents.

Concerned for the enforcement and application by member states of laws and regulations whose extraterritoriality affects the sovereignty of other nations and the legitimate interests of entities or persons within their jurisdiction and the freedom of trade and navigation.

Having full knowledge of the recent enforcement of similar measures aimed at strengthening and widening the economic, commercial and financial blockade against Cuba.

1. Calls on member states to abstain from enforcing or applying laws and measures of the kind referred to in the preamble of the current resolution, in compliance with their obligation to adhere to the Charter and international law and the commitments legally entered into by subscribing to international legal procedures which, among others, recognise the freedom of trade and navigation.

2. Urges nations where these kinds of laws or measures exist to fulfill their legal duty by taking whatever measures are necessary to eliminate or annul their effects as quickly as possible.

3. Requests that the Secretary-General draw up a report [and report] back on compliance with the current resolution for consideration at the 48th session.

4. Decides to include this item for discussion on the provisional agenda of its 48th session.

In favor of the resolution: 59; against: 3; abstentions: 71

Appendix 3

Resolution of the European Parliament on the U.S. "Cuban Democracy Act" (December 1992)

The European Parliament
   Having regard to the Cuban Democracy Act or Torricelli Act adopted by the United States Congress and signed by President Bush,
   Having regard to the United Nations General Assembly Resolution of November 24, 1992, rejecting the Cuban Democracy Act,

   A. **Whereas** this Act unilaterally imposes restrictions on the national sovereignty of other states and constitutes a deliberate, flagrant violation of international law on free trade and freedom of transit. Incompatible with the principles of the EEC-USA Transatlantic Declaration,
   B. **Whereas** in 1991 President Bush rejected a similar proposal, the Mack Amendment, his justification being that the amendment was extraterritorial in character and infringed international law,
   C. **Having regard to** the positions opposing this law adopted by the Commission and the Presidency of the Council of Ministers of the member states of the Community, the governments of Canada and Uruguay and the Parliaments of Mexico, Venezuela, among others,
   D. **Whereas** isolation of a state which has not been decided on by the United Nations can make no contribution to democratization and may, on the contrary, serve as a pretext for harder-line policy,

1. **Supports** the complaint lodged with the U.S. State Department by the Presidency-in-Office of the Council of Ministers of the European Community,
2. **Calls on** the President-Elected of the United States, once he has taken office, and the U.S. Congress to remove from the statute books the Cuban Democracy Act, the extraterritorial nature of which vis-a-vis United States jurisdiction represents a flagrant violation of the international free trade and freedom of transit,
3. **Calls on** the Council, the Commission and the government of the member states to undertake joint action to bring about the annulment of this Act,
4. **Calls on** the Council, the Commission and the government of the member states to step up, via NGOs, their humanitarian aid to the Cuban people,
5. **Instructs** its delegation for the United States to raise this problem at its next meeting with members of Congress,
6. **Instructs** its President to forward this resolution to the Council, the Commission, the governments of the member states, the President and the Cuban authorities.

Appendix 4

Testimony to the U.S. Congressional hearing on U.S.-Cuba policy by Wayne Smith, March 1994

Wayne Smith was head of the U.S. Interests Section in Havana during the Carter Administration, and now teaches at John Hopkins University. The following is excerpted from his testimony to the hearing on Rep. Charles Rangel's HR 2229 (Free Trade with Cuba bill) on March 17, 1994.

The question before us is simple: Is it in the interests of the United States to begin to lift the trade embargo against Cuba and at long last to take other measures to move toward a more constructive relationship with that island?

My answer is an unequivocal "yes." It is indeed in the interests of the United States to take those steps? Why? Because that is the best way to achieve our remaining objectives in Cuba. I say "remaining" because all our foreign policy goals have long since been achieved. We used to say to the Cubans that once they had removed their troops from Africa, once they had stopped intervening in revolutionary situations in Central America and other parts of the world, and once they had significantly reduced their military relationship with our principal global rival, the Soviet Union, that then we could begin to improve relations with them.

Clearly, all those conditions have been fulfilled. That and more. The Soviet Union has collapsed. The Cold War is over. Cuba is no longer a security concern to us or to anyone else. It is prepared to live in peace with its neighbors and to play a constructive role within the international community. But none of that has made any difference. Rather than improving relations as we'd promised, we've actually increased the pressures against Cuba. . . .

Other nations note this profound inconsistency in our policy toward Cuba and conclude that it is driven not by concern for human rights, not by legitimate foreign policy concerns, but by domestic politics. They thus see no reason to support us. "Pander to any tiny percentage of voters in Miami or Union City if you wish," one Canadian diplomat noted some years back, "but don't expect us to share your obsession or follow your lead."

Our Cuba policy is so out of step, so counterproductive, so obviously illogical and flawed, that virtually no other country supports it. Oh yes, Israel votes with us every year in the United Nations General

Assembly not to condemn the embargo, but even Israel trades with Cuba. So does the rest of the world . . .

Our Cuba policy not only isolates us but stands in the way of economic gains. For example, the U.S. government has an obligation to U.S. citizens who lost properties in Cuba back in the 1960s. The Cuban government is prepared to sit down to negotiate a compensation agreement. . . The reason there is no agreement with us is that the U.S. government is not prepared to sit down with the Cubans. . . In effect, it shirks its obligations to its citizens by refusing to come to the bargaining table.

It also does a disservice to American businessmen by closing them out of the Cuban market. Why should they stand by and watch all the trade and profits go to French, Spanish and Canadian businessmen? Estimates are that we could very quickly be doing seven to eight billion dollars a year in trade with Cuba. About half that would be in U.S. exports. In other words, we could be selling at least half as much to Cuba as we are to China, a much larger market but one further away. If we value the one, and we obviously do, why should we be willing to forego the other?. . . .

One argument put forward by supporters of the so-called Cuban Democracy Act was that the fall of the Castro government was imminent. . . Cuba remains in the midst of an acute economic crisis, but there are no signs of collapse. Quite the contrary, there are signs of some slight recovery. Cuban oil production is up; the price of sugar, nickel and other Cuban exports are up, while the price of petroleum is down. More oil is coming in. Energy blackouts have been reduced. A French company is now drilling the first major off-shore oil well. If it comes in, and the prospects look good, that will change the situation significantly. The most likely thing is that the present Cuban government will muddle through. Thus, rather than waiting for an "imminent" collapse that is never likely to take place, the United States should begin to engage with the Cuban government. It should lift the travel controls and begin to trade, even as it makes it clear that movement toward a more open system and greater respect for human rights remain as concerns and will condition how far we can go in a new relationship with Cuba. That is what in our own interests we should do. . . .

[Excerpted from *CUBA Update*, No. 3, 1994]

Appendix 5

The politics of suffering: The impact of the U.S. embargo on the health of the Cuban people

Excerpt from report of a fact-finding trip to Cuba, June 6-11, 1993, by the American Public Health Association.

The past several years have been difficult for the Cuban people. The economies of Cuba's major trading partners have collapsed. The 33-year U.S. embargo was tightened with the passage of the "Cuban Democracy Act" of 1992 to include trade — mostly in food and medicines — by subsidiaries of U.S. companies in other countries. The March 1993 "Storm of the Century," which devastated communities from the Caribbean to Canada, caused an estimated $1 billion in damage to Cuba. A mysterious disease known as neuropathy, which can affect vision, appeared in late 1991 and has spread throughout the island. All this has created a situation of scarcity and uncertainty that has affected all aspects of Cuban society, including its health care system.

The strains on the Cuban economy are visible everywhere. Almost everything, from paper to shampoo, is in short supply. The food supply has diminished, and the Cuban diet is much less adequate than before in both quality and quantity. Medicines of all kinds and medical supplies — from surgical gloves to sutures — are scarce. The lack of eyeglasses has already begun to affect schoolchildren's ability to learn. The huge reduction in the availability of oil has emptied the streets of cars, causes periodic power shortages, disrupted factory production, and increased unemployment and underemployment.

One crucial impact of the U.S. embargo is its interference in Cuba's access to food and medical products. While the lack of hard currency to purchase products is central to Cuba's trade difficulties, even with hard currency Cuba often cannot obtain the necessary goods at any price. U.S. subsidiary trade, 70 percent of which was in food, medicines and medical equipment is now prohibited. Replacement parts and supplies for some of Cuba's high-technology diagnostic equipment are under U.S. patent or are manufactured only by U.S. firms, and are thus inaccessible. Even when medicines and medical supplies can be obtained from sources other than U.S. firms or subsidiaries, transportation and product costs are much higher.

All these difficulties threaten the health of the Cuban people. Cuba entered this period having achieved the health profile of an advanced country. The communicable diseases so rampant in the rest of the developing world have been overcome and have been replaced by chronic diseases such as cancer, heart disease, and diabetes found in the rich countries. Cuba's infant mortality rate and under-5 child mortality rate rival those of advanced industrialized countries. Through a complete restructuring of its health care system after the revolution of 1959, Cuba has developed an exemplary national health system which provides comprehensive, accessible health care to the entire population without charge. Cubans benefit from an abundance of highly skilled doctors and other trained health personnel, who focus on preventative activities and health promotion. Cuba has achieved near universal literacy, and health is an integral part of education and social services.

This strong foundation is central to Cuba's ability so far to avoid the most dire repercussions of the economic crisis. At this time there is no obvious malnutrition. The key health indicators, such as the infant mortality rate and under-5 child mortality rate, are being maintained. There has been no increase to date in the major infectious diseases of childhood. No-one is sleeping in the streets. All children still go to school and the younger ones attend high-quality day care centers.

Cuba has been able to maintain its health system to date only through extraordinary determination and creativity. In spite of their greatest efforts, Cuban health workers are stretched to the limit. They are working long hours in highly stressful circumstances. Physicians and nurses must count every pill and measure every drop of medicine they use. Their ability to further ration scarce resources is extremely limited. While the overall health of the Cuban population has not yet seriously eroded as a result of the economic decline, severe problems threaten to emerge in the future.

The U.S. national grudge against Cuba — exemplified by the recent tightening of the embargo — is out of step with the changes occurring in the world. The policy is damaging to U.S. interests as well as to the wellbeing of the Cuban people. The embargo's interference in the Cuban people's access to food and medicine is tantamount to the use of food and medicine as a weapon in the U.S. arsenal against Cuba. Surely, in this day, with the Cold War behind us, the most powerful nation in the world can devise a policy that does not cause suffering among an entire population in order to accomplish our national political objectives. It is time for a new vision in U.S. policy toward Cuba.

Opponents of the blockade

American Association of Jurists
American Baptist Church
American Hotel and Motel Association
American Public Health Association
Andean Parliament
Edward Asner
Association of Latin American Jurists
Harry Belafonte
Tony Benn
Jackson Browne
Noam Chomsky, MIT
Julie Christie
Ramsey Clark, former U.S. attorney general
Irwin Corey
Ossie Davis
European Community
Evangelical Lutheran Church in America
Gabriel García Márquez
Danny Glover
Stephen Jay Gould
Italian Labor Confederation
Rev. Jesse Jackson
Raúl Julia
Margot Kidder
Kris Kristofferson
Latin American Parliament
Cindy Lauper
Jack Lemmon
Shirley MacLaine
Norman Mailer
Nelson Mandela
Cheech Marin
George McGovern
Robert McNamara
Methodist Church of Great Britain
Mexican Congress
Kate Millet
National Conference of Catholic Bishops
National Council of Churches of Christ
National Lawyers Guild
Holly Near
Robert DeNiro
Nonaligned Nations Movement
Organization of African Unity
Gregory Peck
Sydney Pollack
Robert Redford
Linda Rondstadt
Susan Sarandon
Pete Seeger
Martin Sheen
Wayne Smith, former head of U.S. Interests Section in Havana
Benjamin Spock, MD
Studs Terkel
United Methodist Church
United Presbyterian Church
George Wald, Nobel Prize laureate
Alice Walker
World Council of Churches
Peter Yarrow

Also published by Ocean Press

CRUEL AND UNUSUAL PUNISHMENT
The U.S. blockade against Cuba
by Mary Murray

Is Washington's trade ban with Cuba an embargo, as the U.S. government claims, or an illegal blockade? Does the policy violate international law, the United Nations' Charter and the principles of the Organization of American States? Is it, as Cuba says, one of the worst human rights violatoions ever committed by one country against another? *Cruel and unusual punishment* will help you make up your mind.

THE CUBAN REVOLUTION AND THE UNITED STATES
A chronological history
by Jane Franklin

An invaluable resource for scholars, teachers, journalists, legislators, and anyone interested in international relations, this volume offers an unprecedented vision of U.S.-Cuba relations. *Expanded second edition.*

CUBA: TALKING ABOUT REVOLUTION
Conversations with Juan Antonio Blanco by Medea Benjamin

A frank discussion on the current situation in Cuba, this book presents an all-too-rare opportunity to hear the voice of one of the island's leading intellectuals.

FACE TO FACE WITH FIDEL CASTRO
A conversation with Tomás Borge

One of the most important books to emerge from Latin America in the 1990s, this is a lively dialogue between two of the region's most controversial political figures.

ZR RIFLE
The plot to kill Kennedy and Castro
by Claudia Furiati

Thirty years after the death of President Kennedy, Cuba has opened its secret files on the assassination. These Cuban files show how and why the CIA, through those responsible for its anti-Cuba operations, along with the anti-Castro exiles and the Mafia, planned and orchestrated the Kennedy assassination.

For a list of Ocean Press distributors, see the copyright page

Walks in the
SHADOW OF DARTMOOR

Denis McCallum

OBELISK PUBLICATIONS

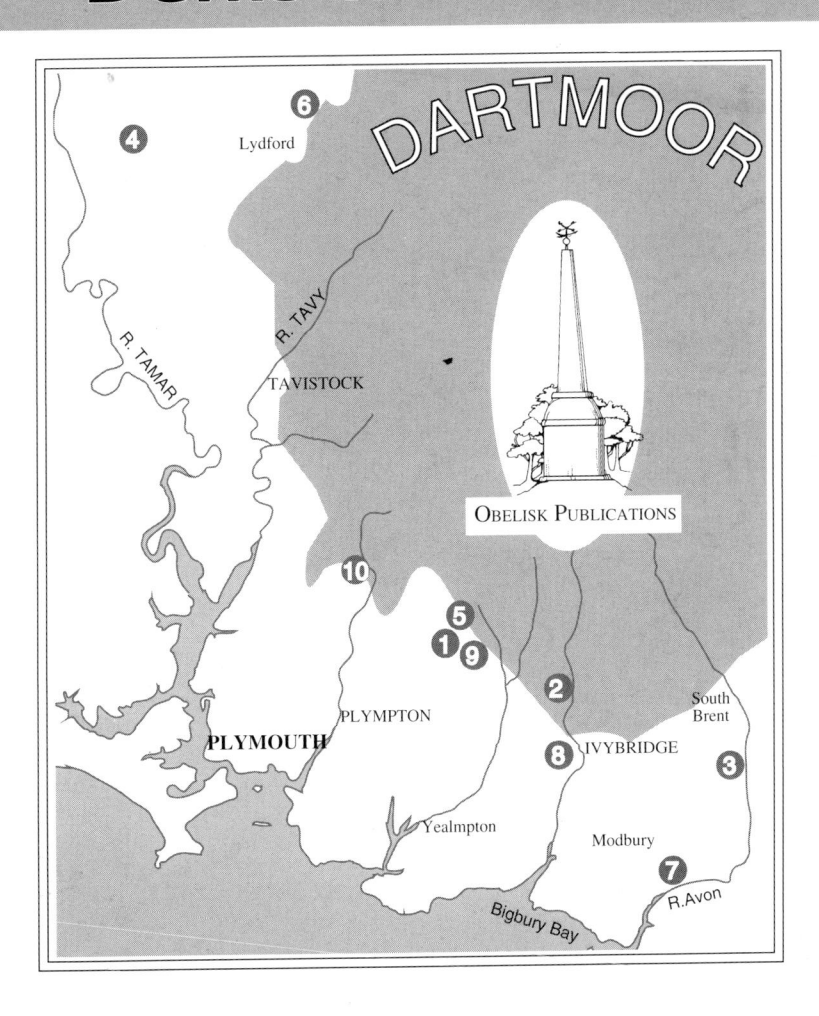

OTHER 'WALKING' TITLES FROM OBELISK PUBLICATIONS INCLUDE:
Walks in Tamar and Tavy Country, Denis McCallum
Walks in the South Hams, Brian Carter
Diary of a Dartmoor Walker, Chips Barber
Diary of a Devonshire Walker, Chips Barber
Ten Family Walks on Dartmoor, Sally & Chips Barber
Ten Family Walks in East Devon, Sally & Chips Barber
The Great Walks of Dartmoor, Terry Bound
Rambling in the Plymouth Countryside, D. Woolley & M. Lister
Walking "with a Tired Terrier" In and Around Torbay, Brian Carter
The Templer Way, Derek Beavis

For further details of any of our titles, please contact us at the address below or telephone Exeter (0392) 68556

PLATE ACKNOWLEDGEMENTS
All sketch maps by Sally Barber based on drawings by the author
Cover photographs by Chips Barber

This book is dedicated to my wife Sheila and our friend Bryan Francis: my thanks for their company on these walks, and for their (sometimes unfounded) faith in my orienteering skills.

First published in 1992 by
Obelisk Publications, 2 Church Hill, Pinhoe, Exeter, Devon
Designed by Sally Barber
Typeset by Sally Barber
Printed in Great Britain by

© **Denis McCallum 1992**
All Rights Reserved

CONTENTS

Introduction .... Page 4

Walk One .... Page 5
    PARK LANE, ELFORDLEIGH – HEMERDON – CROWNHILL DOWN

Walk Two .... Page 8
    IVYBRIDGE – ERME VALLEY – HANGER DOWN

Walk Three .... Page 11
    GARA BRIDGE – CALIFORNIA CROSS – COARSEWELL

Walk Four .... Page 14
    LEE DOWNS – MARYSTOW – CHILLATON – SYDENHAM

Walk Five .... Page 16
    DRAKELAND CORNER/HEMERDON BALL – LUTTON – TOLCHMOOR GATE

Walk Six .... Page 20
    LYDFORD – BRIDESTOWE – FERNWORTHY DOWN

Walk Seven .... Page 23
    AVETON GIFFORD – LODDISWELL

Walk Eight .... Page 25
    IVYBRIDGE – ERMINGTON

Walk Nine .... Page 27
    SMITHALEIGH – LUTTON

Walk Ten .... Page 30
    SHAUGH BRIDGE – CLEARBROOK

INTRODUCTION

Dartmoor is justly popular with both locals and visitors, and there are numerous books on the subject. This isn't one of them.

The area in the shadow of Dartmoor – the "in country" – has always seemed to me just as fascinating as the Moor itself, yet very few books have been written about it, and even fewer "walking books". This is an attempt to redress the balance somewhat, at least as far as the western and southern border country is concerned.

Dartmoor was formed by the intrusion of igneous rock (granite), rather like a gigantic molten fist smashing through the pre-existing strata and pushing them upwards all around it. One of the effects of the extreme heat and pressure accompanying this process was the mineralisation of the original rocks, so that rich deposits of metal ores, mainly tin, copper, arsenic, silver and lead, occur all around the Moor. These have been mined for centuries, but most intensively in the nineteenth century. Also, the granite itself has decayed in places to form kaolin, and this has given rise to the china clay industry. One of the unique attractions of the area is the combination of wonderful scenery and the sense of history you get from these early mining remains, connecting as they do with more modern extractive industries.

Not being all that fond of carting sandwiches and flasks around with me, I have tried to include a pub at an appropriate point on all but one of these walks where you can have lunch, but this is not compulsory! At the start of each walk I try to give you an idea of how steep, muddy and rough it is, and of the distance involved (4 to 7 miles). I have also tried to grade them into easy or moderate – there are no strenuous ones, at least I hope not – but this is pretty risky: so much depends on your physical condition and the state of the paths and bridleways. A walk that would be easy on a dry summer's day might be quite arduous in wet and muddy winter conditions, for which wellies would be virtually essential. In any event you will need stout footwear in all but the driest conditions.

The nature of the terrain means that a certain amount of road walking is unavoidable, but I have tried to restrict this to quiet lanes as far as possible. However, on some of the walks stretches of fairly busy road can't be avoided, and I would urge you to take the greatest care here. Please keep to the public footpaths and bridleways as described: to diverge from them means that you are trespassing. Be sure to shut all gates (unless obviously left open for a purpose), keep dogs under control and avoid dropping litter. End of sermon.

Although the information given in this book is correct to the best of my knowledge at the time of writing, nothing stands still. Rights of way may be diverted or extinguished, new houses and roads are built, pubs stop doing food or close and footpath signs appear (and disappear). Take a map with you (the 1:50 000 OS map at least) to supplement the sketch maps in this book.

Walk One

Park Lane, Elfordleigh – Hemerdon – Crownhill Down

Easy. Park Lane at the start of the walk can be muddy after heavy rain, but the rest is fairly dry. 5¼ miles. OS 1:50 000 Map 202, OS 1:25 000 Map 1356, Outdoor Leisure Map 28.

This walk is through countryside very close to Plymouth but which is nevertheless surprisingly unfrequented, at least on weekdays – I wouldn't recommend it on a fine summer weekend. It does, however, have the disadvantage of including about a mile altogether (in two doses) of fairly busy and narrow road, but unfortunately there is no way of avoiding this at present.

From the Marsh Mills roundabout under the flyover on the A38 in Plymouth, take the B3416 road to Plympton. Turn left at the second set of traffic lights (by the Unicorn pub and a Shell garage) into Larkham Lane. Go on until you reach a T-junction. Turn right here, then immediately left into Crossway. Follow this until you reach another T-junction, where you turn left on to the Shaugh Prior–Cadover Bridge road. Follow this road for about 2 miles past Boringdon Hall (an Elizabethan manor house, now a hotel) and the Elfordleigh Hotel. About 200 yards beyond the Woodside Animal Welfare Centre turn right. A quarter of a mile along this road you will see a wide gateway on your right. There is plenty of room here, so you are unlikely to obstruct the gateway if you park sensibly, but do bear in mind that the track is used by forestry and farm vehicles.

Go through the gateway and straight down the track, ignoring the gate into the plantation on your left. This is Park Lane, which has always been known in my wife's family as "Primrose Lane" for a reason which will be obvious if you do the walk in spring. It is a very pleasant walk at any season, much of it through woodland and most of it downhill. However, it can sometimes be very muddy when churned up by tractors and horses.

From the gateway where you parked you will have seen a solitary chimney stack in the middle of a field. This belonged to Wheal Julian, a tin and arsenic mine which was worked in the heyday of mining in the middle years of the nineteenth century. Further down the track, hidden in the woods, is a similar stack which terminated the arsenic flues of Wheal Sidney, a mine which was worked at the same period but which is on the site of much older workings. The stack is the most obvious relic, but shafts and dumps can be found in the woods nearby.

Park Lane is about one and a half miles long; towards the end it descends fairly steeply towards the Tory Brook valley, through a sort of gully which has been worn down to the bedrock well below the level of the surrounding land by the abrasion of feet, hooves and water over the centuries. It emerges by a lodge at the end of the back drive to the Elfordleigh Hotel, which in turn brings you out on to the main Plympton–Lee Moor road at Loughtor Mill. The latter is at present a garage, but at the side of the building can still be seen the rotting remains of the old wooden mill wheel which drove the machinery when it was a mill: apparently there used to be two wheels.

However, this is no place to indulge in industrial archaeological speculations, as the road is narrow and pretty busy with heavy trucks plying to and from the china clay works at Lee Moor. It is best to hasten over the next hundred yards or so to the comparative security of the raised grass verge on the left of the road, which will take you past the narrowest part. Thereafter revert to normal road-walking practice and transfer to the right-hand side to face the oncoming traffic. There are plans to build a new link road to by-pass this narrow section, but until this happens great care is needed.

The main road leads steadily uphill for about half a mile, with views over Newnham Park to Newnham House on your left. Take the first turning right into a narrow lane which takes you down into a wooded valley and up again into the village of Hemerdon. If going straight on with the walk, take the first turning on the left opposite the telephone kiosk, but if you are calling at the pub, carry straight on for a few yards and you will find it on your right: this is the Miner's Arms, a seventeenth century pub which has been in the same family for several generations, once run as a working farm as well until the demands of the modern licensed trade made this impossible. It is also unusual in having quite a deep well in one of the bars! Real ales and bar snacks may be obtained here.

After leaving the pub, retrace your steps to the telephone kiosk and turn right up the hill out of the village (Galva Road). Three quarters of a mile up this steadily-climbing road you take the first turning on the left, which leads you down into the valley of the Smallhanger Brook (a tributary of the Tory Brook), in which there used to be a number of mines. On the hillside above you to the right may be seen the stack and dumps of the biggest and oldest of these, Bottle Hill. Indeed, the pub is not called "The Miner's Arms" for nothing, as the whole area has been extensively mined right up to the recent past.

The road then climbs out of the valley before dropping down to the Plympton–Lee Moor road again past a scrap yard in an old quarry. The road is much wider here, and you only stay on it for about half a mile.

Just past the cattle grid where the road enters open downland (Crownhill Down), take a track you will see on your left descending into the shallow valley through the gorse bushes. This takes you across the small stream at the bottom, then gently uphill alongside the woodland hedge until it meets the main road again at a point where a minor road turns off it over a cattle grid on the left. Take this turning.

While you have been walking across the down you will have been looking across at ECC International's extensive china clay works on the opposite hillside. The white spoil heaps on the hilltop, some of which have been sown with grass and reclaimed, mark the sites of the actual pits where the clay (degraded granite) is extracted by being washed out of the ground by powerful hoses. The rest of the complex straggling down the hill is concerned with purifying, blending, and separating the clay into various grades and particle sizes. The whole process, on this site at least, terminates in the vast "mica dam" at the bottom of the hill, where the unwanted mica and other heavy particles are settled out. This has grown enormously in recent years with the expansion of the industry, and the company has put a lot of effort into planting trees and landscaping it. The actual clay, which is still suspended in water at this stage, is piped down to the drying plant at Marsh Mills, where it is converted into the final product.

The minor road you now take leads down to a bridge across the Tory Brook, where at 3 a.m. one summer night back in the forties I saw my first badger. You will notice that the water is faintly cloudy. This is because it contains the run-off from the mica dam, but it is vastly better now than it used to be: years ago it used to run as white as milk the whole time. As you climb the hill on the other side of the valley you can look back and see this water running down a stepped cascade from the dam.

The road climbs steadily out of the Tory Brook valley, eventually passing deserted Portworthy farm. The present farmhouse looks as though it was built in the last century, but a very dilapidated building just inside the gate looks far older, to judge from the remains of mullioned windows. My guess is that this was the original farmhouse which was relegated to a barn when the more recent house was built.

Eventually you come to a T-junction at the top of the hill. Turn left here and you will come to where you parked the car in a quarter of a mile.

Walk Two

Ivybridge – Erme Valley – Hanger Down

Fairly easy. Can be muddy after rain in the Erme Valley, but the rest is fairly dry. 4¾ miles. OS 1:50 000 Map 202, OS 1:25 000 Map 1357.

This is a walk through the Dartmoor border country: it takes you up the valley of a moorland river as it makes the transition from moor to in-country, then returns across downland with magnificent views over the South Hams. Unlike most of the other walks, there is no conveniently-placed pub on the route, so you will need a packed lunch unless you decide that it is so short that you could easily do it in a morning or an afternoon with lunch in Ivybridge either before or after.

Ten miles east of Plymouth, turn off the A38 into Ivybridge and drive up through the main street. When you come to the end of the shops, turn left opposite a pub called the Exchange just before the "new bridge", and drive along beside the river Erme. In 100 yards you reach a crossroads by the Constitutional Club and the old "Ivy Bridge". There is a village tradition that to be a real local you must have fallen fully-clothed into the river between these two bridges – and I qualify! Go straight on alongside the Erme's western bank. Just past the iron gates of the paper mill the road swings left and forks. Take the right-hand turning and carry on up the hill and under the viaduct. A hairpin bend just after this leads up towards the site of the old station, where there is ample room to park. Be careful not to obstruct the track which goes on up the hill, as this is in constant use.

Walk back down the hill, then just past the viaduct turn sharp left through a gateway on to a track which leads down towards the river. You pass under the viaduct yet again – on the upstream side of it you will observe a line of twin granite piers following the same curve. These supported Brunel's original viaduct, built in the mid-nineteenth century to carry the broad-gauge line to Plymouth. It had a timber superstructure on top of the piers, and I believe was the first viaduct to be built on a curve. It was replaced by the present granite structure early this century.

The track now runs beside the river, and a little further on you will come to a weir (Head Weir) with a hatch and leat intake on the other bank. This is where the 200-year-old Stowford Paper Mill abstracts its water supply. I worked there for 23 years and, as part of my job was concerned with water usage and treatment, I used to walk up to the intake about once a day. During my first ten or eleven years there I quite often saw otters swimming in the river or leat, or just pottering around the river bank. They are lovely creatures, very amusing and endearing to watch: like some rare people, they light up the world around them and raise the spirits. Sadly, it is many years since I have seen one in the area. The reason, of course, is the increase in human activity: Ivybridge 25 years ago was a quiet little mill town with a very rural atmosphere – now it is expanding rapidly. Whereas in those days one hardly ever saw anyone on the riverside path, it is now a favourite dog-walking area, so no more otters, just the occasional mink. It is similar to what has happened to the numbers of song birds near towns: they seem to have been largely replaced by magpies, crows and jackdaws. This is just one of the many prices we pay for the suburbanisation of the countryside: we get the wildlife we deserve.

A little further on you will see a large concrete basin on your left, locally known as "the swimming pool". This was a reservoir constructed by the American servicemen who were stationed here during the Second World War.

The broad, well-defined track ends at a ladder stile. Climb this and carry on along the path beside the river, which is now much narrower and muddy in places – at one point a boggy patch is crossed by stepping "stones" made from sections of tree trunk. Shortly after this point you come to a stile into a field, and the path then crosses the bottom of this to another stile. Over this second stile is a streamlet – after you cross this the path bears to the right, down to the river bank. Indeed, it gets very close to the river in a couple of places, where you have to squeeze past tree trunks and over their roots on the bank. If the river is very high it may be difficult or impossible to get past here: you may have to make a detour up to the left over the rough boggy ground away from the path. The river Erme, like any Dartmoor river, is an awesome sight when it is in spate – a wide brown sinewy torrent roaring down the full width of its bed and right up to the top of its banks, indeed over them in places. In all my years at the mill, however, I never actually caught the moment when "the flood came down", which I'm told occurs with startling suddenness: the river rises steadily throughout a period of heavy rain, then, presumably at the point when the peat on the moor above becomes saturated, a wall of water like the Severn bore is supposed to come down, usually when the weather is clearing. Stay well away from the river when it's in this state: if you fell in you would have no chance at all.

The path continues beside the river, over a couple of cornditch-type walls with projecting stone steps, over a wooden footbridge and through a strip of scattered woodland. It then bears left away from the river (as indicated by the signpost), crosses a shallow ford over a little stream, and starts to climb the hill. Follow the wire fence on your right – where the path enters a field you will see a small gate on your right. Go through this, and you descend through an area of scrubland and scattered trees with fine views across the Erme valley to Harford church and Hangershell Rock on the moor above. After crossing a small stream, the path then climbs slightly to a gate into a plantation. Go through this and continue up to the gate at the top of the wood, which leads into a field. There are often sheep here, so keep dogs under control.

Turn right and walk along beside the hedge. Then go through a gap into another field, which you cross diagonally to the left to reach a gate at the bottom. This gives access to a rough lane between stone walls which takes you up on to the narrow Harford–Cornwood road.

Turn left and follow the road, which is a very quiet one, for about half a mile until you come to another rough track leading off to the left through an avenue of beeches. This takes you out on to Hanger Down. Make for the beech hanger you will see in front of you: this is a landmark for miles around, so as you might expect, there are magnificent views of southern Dartmoor and out over the South Hams from here. One early spring day I was with a group of people near here when we came across a sick ewe with her lamb crying piteously beside her. Some of the party volunteered to go to the nearest farm and alert the farmer. When they got there the farmer asked what sort of sheep it was: the spokesman was somewhat taken aback, and replied, "A woolly one!" The farmer's reaction is not recorded, but eventually the right owner was contacted.

From Hanger Down Clump, walk south-south-east towards Ivybridge, keeping parallel to the wall surmounted by a wire fence you will shortly see on your right. At about the same time a small eminence should come into view in front of you: this is a turf-covered service reservoir at the edge of the down. Make for this, and when you reach it the entrance to a drove lane will be apparent on your right, where the hedges funnel inwards. This lane brings you out on to Henlake Down above Ivybridge. Take the right-hand track nearest the hedge – this will bring you around the edge of the down to two gateways in the bottom corner of the down. Take the left-hand gateway with the wooden gate: this leads into the woods above the old Ivybridge station. Follow the path down through the woods and under a bridge beneath the service road to a house called "Long Timbers" after Longtimber Wood in the Erme valley, through which you passed at the start of the walk. You will emerge on the old approach road to the station, where you left your car.

WALK THREE
GARA BRIDGE – CALIFORNIA CROSS – COARSEWELL

Moderate. Entails a steep climb of 570 feet at the outset. Includes one very muddy, rough stretch and another section through riverside woods which can be muddy after rain. The rest is along roads, very quiet country lanes for the most part. 6¾ miles. OS 1:50 000 Map 202, OS 1:25 000 Outdoor Leisure Map 20.

Turn off the A379 Plymouth–Kingsbridge road on to the B3207 to Dartmouth just before entering Modbury, if travelling from the Plymouth direction. This road turns sharp right in about three and a half miles at California Cross, opposite a pub called the California Inn – don't go straight on here or you will finish up near South Brent. Continue down to the bottom of the hill. Just before coming to the very narrow Gara Bridge itself, you will see a wide entry to some cottages on your left. There is limited parking here, or you can turn right immediately before the bridge – the start of the walk – and park on the verge some way up the hill. If you do this, bear in mind that although you will have avoided that bit of the climb now you will have to do it at the end! If you do this walk out of season, check with the California Inn before leaving to see if they are open if you want a pub lunch: they close on weekday lunchtimes in the winter, as I found to my cost one Monday in January.

Assuming you park just above Gara Bridge, walk down towards it and take the road on the right immediately before it. This runs along by the Avon for a short distance – just before you start to climb you will see one of the steel bridges which used to carry the South Brent–Kingsbridge branch line over the river. From now on it is all uphill for one mile.

Half a mile up this hill you will pass one drive leading down to Hazelwood House in the valley, and another a little further on. The latter is notable for the style in which the walls on either side of it are built: curious arched recesses are built into them, and pillars crowned with lumps of white stone punctuate the walls at regular intervals. You will already have passed another example of this in a drive to a house on the right further down the hill.

From the upper drive to Hazelwood House there are marvellous views north to Western and Eastern Beacons on the southern tip of Dartmoor above South Brent, and to the south to Loddiswell and towards Kingsbridge.

When you reach the top of the hill you will see on your left beside the road the oval outer earth rampart of an ancient fortification called Blackdown Camp, or Loddiswell Rings. This is an Iron-age hill fort which was re-fortified by the Normans. It has lately been opened to the public.

You now descend gently to join the Loddiswell road at Coldharbour Cross – this is the only fairly busy bit of road on the walk. Turn right, and you will arrive at California Cross (again) in three quarters of a mile.

From California Cross take the B3207 opposite the pub, as you did with the car, and in a quarter of a mile turn left on to a minor road. In a further quarter of a mile,

11

just after a road joins from the right, you will see a rough lane leading uphill to the left. Take this and follow it to the top of the hill: this stretch is extremely muddy when churned up by tractors in the winter. The track then drops fairly steeply into the valley: this too is muddy, and very rough and uneven. Go through a gate at the bottom where it crosses a stream, and follow the lane up the opposite hillside: this is much better underfoot and not as steep as the descent, but there is still a very muddy stretch just before you reach Coarsewell.

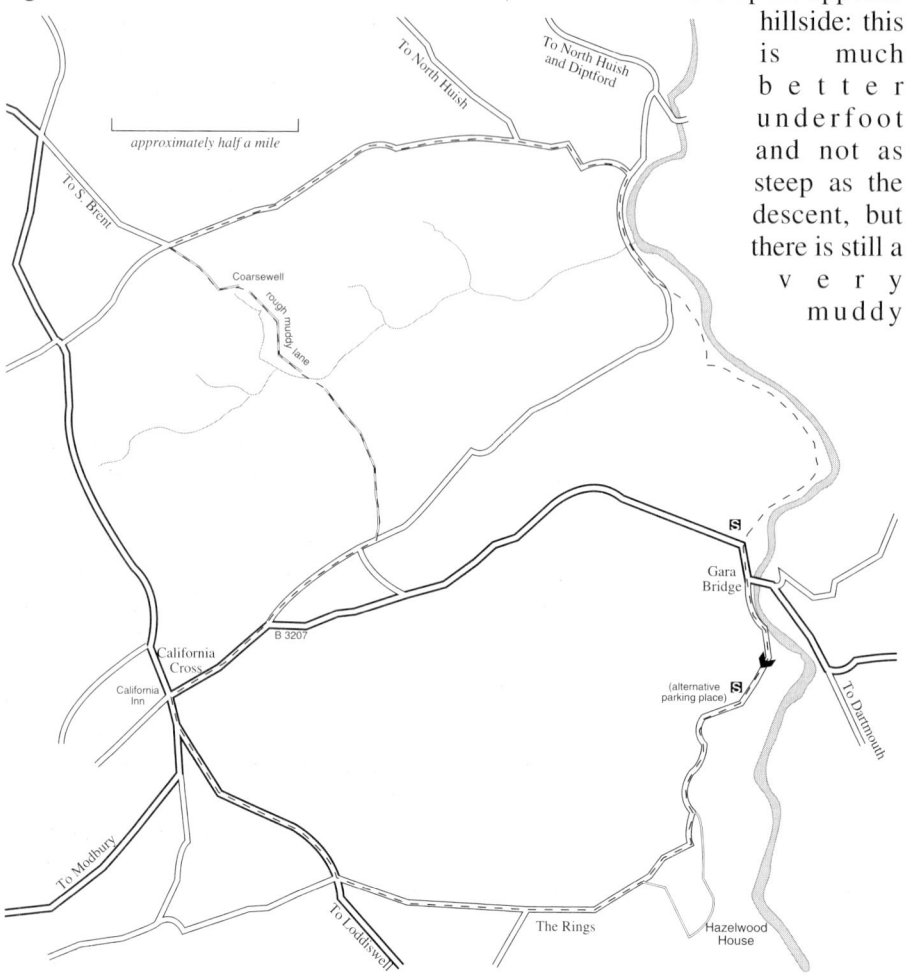

Follow the road up through this tiny settlement to the crossroads at the top and turn right for Clunkamoor. On our last visit here we met a delightful little black-and-white collie cross bitch, who decided she was going to accompany us and was completely impervious to all efforts to dissuade her. When we reached the crossroads at the top I decided that that was far enough, as I certainly didn't want her loose on the road. So I took her back down the lane to near where she joined us and told her sternly to "stay", walking backwards away from her and staring

12

at her commandingly, as I thought. This seemed to work as she got interested in some roadside smells and eventually disappeared into the drive of a nearby house. That's that, I thought, and hastened back up the lane to join the others. But we had only gone 400 yards along the road when she appeared beside us again. This was now a real dilemma: you always tend to think that when a dog reaches the limit of its territory it will turn back, but sometimes it doesn't, as in this case. She had obviously adopted us as family, and assumed we would be returning with her to her home after an enjoyable walk, as usual. "I'm going to walk her back," I said after about a mile. "What's the point?" said our friend Bryan, "You don't know where she lives exactly and there's nobody about in Coarsewell to leave her with: she'll only follow you back here again." I agreed that that was quite likely, so we decided to let her follow us back to the car and then drive her back to Coarsewell to find her owner, who should be back by then. I therefore improvised a dog lead out of a length of ivy.

So this pretty little bitch with the lovely brown eyes danced gaily on down the hill in front of us, ears pricked, tail waving, to the T-junction at the bottom, where you turn right to walk along beside the river Avon. In a quarter of a mile, just where the road starts to climb out of the valley, a footpath sign points into the woods on the left – this is the path you want. It is a very picturesque woodland walk following the Avon back down to Gara Bridge: here the dog really started to enjoy herself, chasing smells all over the woodlands and asking us to throw sticks for her, at which we all took turns. "The rewarding thing about dogs," remarked Bryan, "Is their transparent delight in a walk or a game." I saw what he meant. We were somewhat abashed, however, when we went through a gate and saw a notice on the other side: "Private Shoot: keep dogs on lead". It was a bit late by then.

I put her on her "lead" when we reached the car, and she stood there quietly while we changed out of our muddy boots. She willingly entered the car and went trustingly to sleep on the floor as I drove back to Coarsewell. We encountered the school bus as we reached the bottom of the lane, so guessed that there would now be someone at home. So it proved: the first person we met directed us to the right house, and the lady to whom she belonged didn't even know she was missing, except that she had just been calling her without response. "You silly dog," she said.

Maybe the new laws on stray dogs will prevent this sort of thing happening, but somehow I doubt it, and it's always a bit difficult to know what to do: the first rule, I suppose, is not to be too friendly, but if they follow you anyway the best thing is to lead them firmly back to where they have come from before you get too far away. If, as in this case, there is no one at home to leave them with, or you don't know where they come from, then you have a problem, and I suppose the only answer is to do what we did, as indeed we have had to do on other occasions. What you certainly **don't** do is to drive away and abandon them miles from home. If all else fails, ring the local Police, ask their advice, and hope they don't accuse **you** of allowing the dog to stray!

Walk Four

Lee Downs – Marystow – Chillaton – Sydenham

Easy. The track up to Marystow is usually wet and muddy, but the other off-road sections are usually fairly dry except after heavy rain. 5 miles. OS 1:50 000 Map 201, OS 1:25 000 Map 1327 (SX48/58).

From Bedford Square in Tavistock, go straight across the mini roundabout and up the hill on the Chillaton–Lewtrenchard road (Drake Road). About one and a half miles beyond Chillaton the road crosses the River Lyd, and a few yards beyond this point a minor road turns off on the left along the Lyd valley for Sydenham and Portgate. Go along this road for almost a mile then take the first road on the right. Follow this to the top of the hill, where you will see a footpath sign on your right (ignore the first footpath sign you pass lower down the hill). Park at a suitable spot by the roadside here, but be careful not to obstruct any gateways: obviously you don't park in them, or even opposite them, as farm machinery needs all the room it can get when entering or leaving fields.

Return to the footpath sign and go through the gate into the field. Follow the left-hand hedge along the edge of the field to a double steel gate. Go through this and turn sharp right, following the right-hand hedge to a wooden gate into some woodlands. The track through these woods eventually starts to drop towards the Lyd valley, and is joined by two other tracks ascending from the right. Ignore both of these for the moment, continue along the track you are on. This will bring you out into a disused quarry in which stands the wooden skeleton of what was presumably once a stone-grading plant. This area is known as Lee Downs.

Retrace your steps from the quarry and branch off left in a few yards (along the last of the two tracks you passed on the way down). In a few more yards branch off left again down a stony track which soon bears around to the right and continues downhill. This will bring you out on to another forestry track: turn right, slightly uphill at first, then follow this track until it brings you out on the Lyd valley road you drove along earlier.

Turn right and go along the road for 100 yards until you come to a turning on your left: this takes you down past a house and across a bridge over what used to be the old Tavistock–Launceston branch line to another bridge over the River Lyd (Marystow Bridge). From here the track is unsurfaced and often very wet and muddy as it climbs steeply up towards Marystow. From a gate halfway up this hill there are magnificent views of north Dartmoor.

The track emerges on to the road near Marystow church: follow it around the church and turn right at the T-junction, then almost immediately left. This lane brings you to the main Lewtrenchard–Chillaton road: turn right and follow it into Chillaton, where you may well decide to patronise the Chichester Arms for lunch.

From Chillaton, take the Lifton road opposite the pub and in half a mile take the first turning right. Cross the bridge over the stream in 100 yards, then turn immediately left for Sydenham. This road climbs gently for a quarter of a mile, then drops down to Sydenham past the oddly-named Stewardry Cross.

The imposing Sydenham House is one of the finest examples of an Elizabethan mansion in this area, set in a beautiful spot in the Lyd valley. It was built by Sir Thomas Wise, who also built a house at Plymouth just across the Tamar from Mount Edgcumbe which he called "Mount Wise" – a clear case of keeping up with the Edgcumbes. Although this latter house has long gone the area is still known as Mount Wise. Sydenham House's leaded semicircular windows are an unusual feature, and the stable yard and mews are also worth a look as you pass.

Just before reaching the house you will see an ancient cob wall which is proof of the old saying that cob "needs a good hat and shoes": although obviously repaired here and there, most of it has been preserved for centuries by its stone foundations and slate topping.

Cross the bridge over the river, and another over what was once the old Launceston branch line, then turn left at the T-junction. Here you will see a sign indicating a footpath on your right: ignore this, as it involves a quite unnecessary climb and descent, and continue along the road for a hundred yards or so until you see a gate on your right with a track leading into the woods. This is the one you want. I think this is the pleasantest part of the walk: the track climbs gently up through the wooded valley then bears away to the east opposite the hamlet of Dippertown, still following the valley with a narrow strip of woodland alongside. When you reach the road, turn right and you should soon come to your car. From here there are good views ranging from Dartmoor in the east to Bodmin Moor in the west. The traffic on the A30 can be seen about a mile to the North. The village in the valley is Lifton.

15

Walk Five

Drakeland Corner/Hemerdon Ball – Lutton – Tolchmoor Gate

Fairly easy. Mostly open moorland and moorland tracks, wet and muddy in places after rain. Includes a 300 foot climb on a fairly busy road. 6 miles. OS 1:50 000 Map 202, OS 1:25 000 Map 1356 and Outdoor Leisure Map 28.

This is a walk through the heart of Dartmoor's china clay district. This area, although ravaged by mining activity past and present (particularly present), nevertheless possesses a certain appeal.

From the Marsh Mills roundabout and flyover on the A38 on the outskirts of Plymouth, take the B3416 for Plympton. In about one and a quarter miles, after passing two sets of traffic lights, you come to a mini roundabout by St. Mary's church. Turn left here, carry straight on along Glen Road at another mini roundabout with traffic lights just around the corner (**don't** turn left over the railway bridge) and continue to the first roundabout a short distance beyond the Fire Station. Turn left here into Strode Road, and when you reach the roundabout at the end, turn right. You are now on the Hemerdon–Sparkwell–Cornwood road. Ignore the turning to Lee Moor on the left a couple of hundred yards further along and bear right up the hill. At the top of the hill (in about a mile) you will see a turning on the left signposted "Hemerdon": take this, bear left at the junction 100 yards down the lane, and you come into Hemerdon village, which we visited on foot in Walk One. Pass the Miner's Arms then turn right up the hill by the phone box (Galva Road). Continue up this road for about one mile, passing the turning to Bottle Hill on your left. Continue on to the end of the road, where there is ample room to park at Drakeland Corner. However, be careful not to obstruct any gates or entries.

From here you have two alternatives: you can either walk up through the old Hemerdon Ball mine workings, or head straight on up the track across the down. If you decide on the mine route, walk back down the road to the last Public Footpath sign you passed on the way up (**not** the one nearest Hemerdon village). Turn left and go up the concrete track as indicated by the sign, then go through the gateway on the left at the top, the one with the large red mail box on the gatepost. Don't take too much notice of the old sign which says "Warning: Do Not Enter – Guard Dogs On Patrol". The only "guard dog" we ever met here was delighted to see us and asked us to throw sticks for it! In any case, the public footpath passes through the old mine buildings.

The footpath route through the mine site used to be very confusing, and the OS maps are not much help. However, it has now been well marked with large yellow signs. As directed by these, follow the concrete road past the derelict buildings and the South West Security offices, which are in use. Bear left around the end of the offices, then right, and continue uphill until the road forks. Turn left here, then just where the concrete surface ends a few yards up this road, turn left again along a gravel track.

You now find yourself in a sort of moon landscape: the ground has been extensively excavated and one or two covered-over shafts can be seen. Don't go exploring: it can be dangerous, and you are after all on private property even though the right-of-way passes through it. Wolfram, the ore of tungsten, was last mined here during the forties, and a huge overhead cableway, which could be seen for miles, used to run around the site. There are plans to re-start mining here eventually.

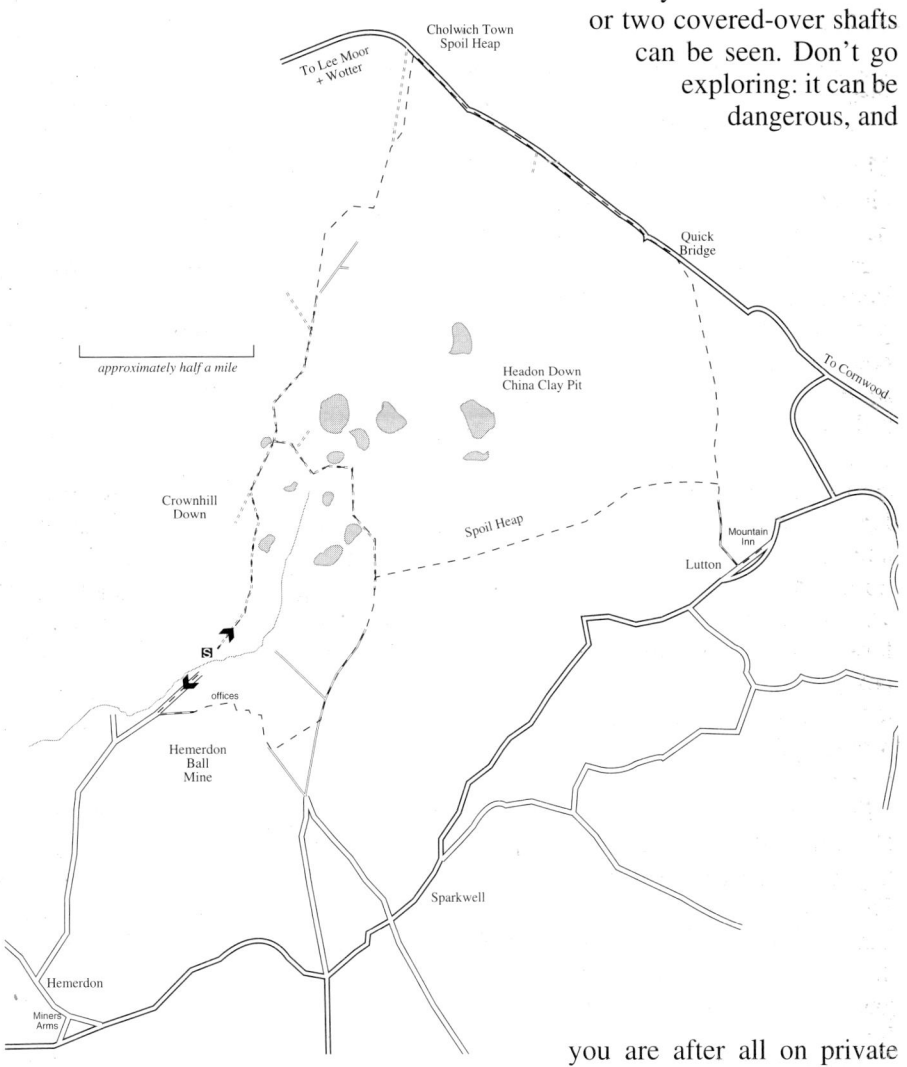

The footpath now does some rather peculiar things: about 100 yards along the gravel road you will see another of the yellow footpath signs pointing up a track leading uphill on the right. Go up this – in a few yards another (unmarked) track branches off to the left towards the hedge. This leads to a stile into a field. Cross the field diagonally to the left to another stile in the far corner. This brings you out where the gravel road you were just walking along joins a lane! It would be far simpler to just continue along this road, but unlike the footpath this is not a public right of way.

Although there are footpath signs and a stile inviting you to enter the field opposite the end of the mine road, you will find it much easier to turn left and follow the lane. Eventually the tarmac surface peters out and the last part of the lane leading to the moorgate can be very muddy. Go through the gate and turn right across the moor alongside the field wall on your right. When this ends, continue in the same easterly direction, steering a slightly downhill course which gradually drops away from the long spoil-heap to your left, which consists of waste from Headon Clay Pit on the other side.

If you choose the other route from Drakeland Corner, cross the wooden bridge over the stream and carry on up the white gravel track across Crownhill Down. In about three quarters of a mile, take another track which branches off to the right just under an old waste heap overgrown with gorse bushes. Don't take any of the other, fainter tracks that turn off right before you get to this waste heap, or you will find yourself in the maze of old clay and mineral workings which fill this little valley and which can be tricky to get through. We tried it once in heavy rain – never again!

Follow the main track around the head of the valley, along by the foot of the huge spoil heap, ignoring minor ones which strike off in all directions. The only other major tracks lead into Headon Clay Pit, and are well signposted with signs saying "WBB – Safety Notice – Quarry – No Admittance". On your left you will see an abandoned clay pit filled with beautiful azure water – the amazing colour is due to the light-scattering effect of the clay particles in it. There is also an old chimney made of granite blocks topped with brickwork, a relic of earlier workings. Above you, modern dumper trucks grind uphill carrying spoil to the top of the heap. Eventually the track climbs up on to open downland and joins up with the other route from Hemerdon mine at the moorgate.

Carry on across the moor as described earlier – when you pass a wooded area to your right continue heading downhill in the general direction of Cornwood church, which you will see in the distance. Eventually, about a mile from the moorgate, you should pick up a track which leads down across a narrowing neck of moorland towards the houses of Lutton. This track leads in turn into an unsurfaced lane. Turn right, cross the cattle grid, and descend the lane into Lutton. Continue straight downhill in the village past the end of Chipple Park. At the T-junction at the bottom of the lane, turn left and in a hundred yards or so you come to the Mountain Inn on your left.

In the area covered by this book there are numerous delightful pubs, but this one is certainly my favourite: I celebrated my retirement here a few years ago. It is very small, consisting of two old cottages knocked into one plus a small recently-built extension. There is, thankfully, no juke box and no anodyne muzak oozing from holes in the wall, just a harmonium in an old fireplace. There is no beeping electronic till, either. The furniture is good, solid, old-fashioned stuff and the beams are genuine. It is still, miraculously, what many country pubs used to be, in which you felt that you were in someone's front parlour. There is no sign of plastic brewery tat, and no pseudo-antiques to give the place "character", since it has it in abundance already. It is a free house noted for real ales and home-cooked food. In winter a log fire burns in the open grate, whilst in summer there is nothing finer than to sit outside on the vine-shaded terrace with a pint, a bowl of their delicious soup and a hunk of Stilton, enjoying the view across the Yealm valley towards Hanger Down.

The only drawback of lunching at the Mountain is that you then have to retrace your steps back up the steep hill to the moor, which takes the gilt off somewhat. From the cattle grid at the top, follow the unsurfaced lane into a plantation. In the valley below you can see the imposing Delamore House, whilst looming ahead of you is the mountainous bulk of the Cholwich Town Clay Pit spoil-heap. The track emerges from the plantation and descends across the moor towards the Cornwood–Lee Moor road, which it joins about a mile from the pub.

Now begins the worst part of this walk: it is a drag in every sense, for from the entrance to Watts Blake Bearne's Headon Clay Works at Quick Bridge you have to follow this fairly busy road for a mile as it climbs 300 feet to Tolchmoor Gate: because of the clay works on either side there is unfortunately no way of avoiding this, but there are verges you can walk along in places. Be very careful on this stretch.

When you reach the top of this hill, you will be right under Cholwich Town spoil-heap – you will notice that while the lower part is well covered by vegetation the upper parts are less so. Years ago the waste gravel from the extraction of clay was simply piled up in a conical mound by means of little trucks hauled up a tramway to the top of these "pyramids". It took many years for plant life to colonise these tips, for as soon as a seed settled, germinated and started to put down roots, the unstable gravel would shift and uproot it, or the rain would wash it away. With modern clay production, also, the volume of waste is far greater, and no way could it be piled into pyramids: it had to be spread out over a wide area, and terraced to stabilise it. But how could these mountains of glaring white gravel be harmonised with the landscape?

The answer involved co-operation between ECC International and the Wiggins Teape (as it then was) paper mill at Ivybridge, where I used to work. Some bright spark in ECC had the idea of suspending seeds in paper mill sludge and spraying this on to the spoil-heap surface. This sludge is produced by the mill effluent treatment plant, and consists mainly of a suspension in water of settled-out cellulose fibre and china clay: what it does is to stabilise the loose gravel surface long enough for plants to establish themselves before the weather erodes it away.

You can see this happening at Cholwich Town: the thinner growth towards the summit indicates that this area has most recently been sprayed with the sludge-seed mixture and the grass, etc. is just becoming established. So every spring and autumn (the planting seasons) for the last few years that I worked there I used to get frequent calls from ECC: "Could we please have 5,000 gallons of sludge tomorrow morning?" We were glad to be rid of it – it was the only practical use we ever found for the stuff!

At the top of the hill you will see a gate on your left – Tolchmoor Gate. Go through it and follow the track across the moor. It eventually joins up with a gravel road leading to a weighted hunting gate, then through another one a hundred yards or so further on. After that there is a fairly steep climb up a hillock alongside the field wall, and another thereafter. From here you will have a grandstand view of Watts Blake Bearne's Headon Clay Pit on your left and ECC's works on your right. The latter consist of three pits: Cholwich Town, Lee Moor and Whitehill Yeo, which cover most of the moor to the north and east. Below these are the settlement tanks (refiners) and other plant for treating the extracted clay.

After you climb the last hillock, you should see a track leading from the farm which you will have seen on your left. Make for this and follow it back to Drakeland Corner.

Many people are outraged by the damage to the landscape caused by large-scale mining and quarrying (as at Headon Clay Pit) and similar industrial enterprises which have a considerable environmental impact – I must admit I was quite concerned about the proposed resumption of mining at Hemerdon, for example. However, I can envisage even the huge craters and waste-mountains of the clay works eventually becoming an extremely attractive landscape with a great deal of archaeological interest, like the abandoned mines which abound in this area. The message to environmentalists is don't worry: everything comes to an end, and time and nature will heal all wounds.

WALK SIX

LYDFORD – BRIDESTOWE – FERNWORTHY DOWN

Easy. Along quiet lanes, metalled and unmetalled. There is one patch which can be wet and rather muddy where a stream overflows across the track. 6¾ miles. OS 1:50 000 Map 191, OS 1:25 000 Map 1327 (SX 48/58).

Turn off the A386 Tavistock–Okehampton road for Lydford opposite the Dartmoor Inn. Turn right by the war memorial just as you enter the village and park on the rough ground where the road forks a few yards further on.

Lydford was once a place of considerable importance and evil repute: the forest law was administered at Lydford Castle in days gone by, and those who offended, or were even suspected of offending, against it were incarcerated in the castle in dreadful conditions and frequently hanged. "Lydford Law" was a synonym for injustice, as it was said that these courts had a way of hanging people first and sitting in judgement afterwards.

As Lydford parish covered so much of the northern moor, anyone who died anywhere within its remote fastnesses had to be carried to Lydford for burial along the Lich Way which runs all the way from Bellever across some pretty inhospitable country, also over rivers prone to flash floods. One can only speculate at what those old corpse-carriers had to endure and marvel at their hardiness.

Take the right-hand road for Watergate, which you reach in about one and a half miles. Turn right here and follow the steadily-climbing road along the edge of Beara Down. From here you have magnificent views of the western heights of north Dartmoor. Looking from north to south, these are Arms Tor, Brat Tor (with Widgery Cross on its summit), and Doe Tor at around 1500 feet. Behind them are Great Links Tor, Chat Tor, Sharp Tor and Hare Tor at 1750 to 1900 feet.

You will come to the B3278 Shortacombe–Bridestowe road in one mile – although it is somewhat busier than the lanes you have been walking you will be unfortunate to encounter more than half-a-dozen cars between here and Bridestowe. Turn left here and you will reach the village in about three quarters of a mile. Note the old well in the wall on your right as you enter the village. You have a choice of two pubs for lunch: the White Hart which you come to first or the Royal Oak opposite the church.

After lunch, take the road which turns off opposite the church, on your right if you are coming from the White Hart, on your left just beside the pub if you are coming from the Royal Oak. Follow this road for a mile past a caravan site and then uphill until you come to a road turning off on your right at the top. From here you can see the traffic on the A386 about 100 yards away below you, whilst beyond the moor heaves steeply up to the majestic height of Corn Ridge, with Sourton Tors on its shoulder to the north-west. Between the moor and the main road can be seen Lake viaduct, which once carried the Southern Region main line from Plymouth to Waterloo over two stream valleys on the flank of the moor.

Take the road on the right, which leads down to the hamlet of Lake on the main road. You don't go as far as that, though, for in about 25 yards you will see a Public Footpath sign pointing down an unsurfaced track on the right. Follow this down into a shallow valley, where the track divides into two: the right-hand branch leads to a very picturesque cottage whilst the left-hand one leads over a ford. The one you want is obviously the one over the ford, but there is no need to get your feet wet: if you go towards the cottage for a few yards on the right-hand track you will come to a stone bridge over the stream taking you back on to the left-hand track.

Continue up the hill from the ford. At the top are two delightfully-situated houses on either side of the track, which after a level stretch descends gradually to the point where it meets the B3278. Cross this road and go on following the track. After a while it gets quite wet where a stream overflows across it for a short distance.

Eventually you come to a gate with a yellow arrow directing you straight on through another gate on to Fernworthy Down. The gate leading into the track on the right leads to Fernworthy and Beara Farms before coming out on the road beside Beara Down which you followed on the way to Bridestowe.

An unfenced track now skirts Fernworthy Down bringing you to a ford with a footbridge beside it. Cross this and go through the gate. A little way up the track a footpath sign indicates another turning up to the left. Take this – after a steepish climb you will emerge on to the road. Turn left, and you will come to where you left your car in about a quarter of a mile.

Walk Seven

Aveton Gifford – Loddiswell

Moderate. Along quiet lanes, footpaths and bridleways with some steep climbs. Muddy in places. 5 miles. OS 1:50 000 Map 202, OS 1:25 000 Map 1362 and Outdoor Leisure Map 20.

Take the A379 Plymouth–Kingsbridge road to Aveton Gifford and park in the car park by the roundabout at the end of the bypass.

The "Aveton" part of Aveton Gifford causes some pronunciation problems:

> Years ago they taught 'en
> To say Auton
> But nowadays they rabbit on
> About Av-et-on

I suppose the reason is that the river Avon used to be called the Aune, hence the name of the village would have been Auneton, shortened to Auton. Now that Avon is the commoner name, it has become Avonton, or Aveton. That's my theory, anyway.

From the car park, go through the little underpass signposted "Village Centre" and walk up the main street. This was part of the main A379 to Kingsbridge before the bypass was built, so you can imagine how chaotic it used to be, especially in summer. Opposite the Weslyan chapel turn right up Rock Hill, quite a steep climb. At the top you will see a footpath sign and a stile: climb this and follow the right-hand hedge to another stile. Climb this then cross the field, aiming to the left of the farm building you see in front of you. From these fields there are terrific views down the Avon estuary and over the flood plain across which the river meanders. Eventually you come to a gate and a modern stile into the road you just left, but the footpath saves a little bit of gradient.

Turn right to follow the road along beside the river past Knap Mill. In a mile you come to Hatch Bridge where you take the rough lane striking off uphill to your left. A short way up this you will see a stone stile on your right: there was a footpath sign here but at the time of writing it had been broken off. Go over the stile and climb steeply up the field to the top right-hand corner. Go through the gap then follow the left-hand hedge, still climbing. Go through the gateway and straight across the next field to a stile, which you will be glad to know marks the end of the climb. Follow the right-hand hedge across the next three fields and stiles until you reach the lane into Loddiswell.

Turn right here, then left through the main street of the village – you will come to the Loddiswell Inn, where you can obtain bar snacks, or more elaborate meals if you wish.

After lunch, carry on uphill past the pub on the main California Cross road for a quarter of a mile until you come to a spot where three roads join from the left at a sort of triangle. Take the third of these for Alleron and Fernhill. Follow this road down into the valley for a mile, ignoring the turnings on the right for Tunley, Fernhill and Alleron House. Just after you cross the stream at the bottom of the valley you should see a Public Bridleway sign pointing through a gate on the left. Go through the gate and follow the bridlepath across a field by the stream to a hunting gate. We found the going a bit rough after this, as we had to force our way through rampant brambles and nettles, probably because a fallen tree halfway along had denied access to horses, which would otherwise have kept it clear. As we were wearing shorts on that occasion we found it pretty uncomfortable. However, it may well have been cleared since then.

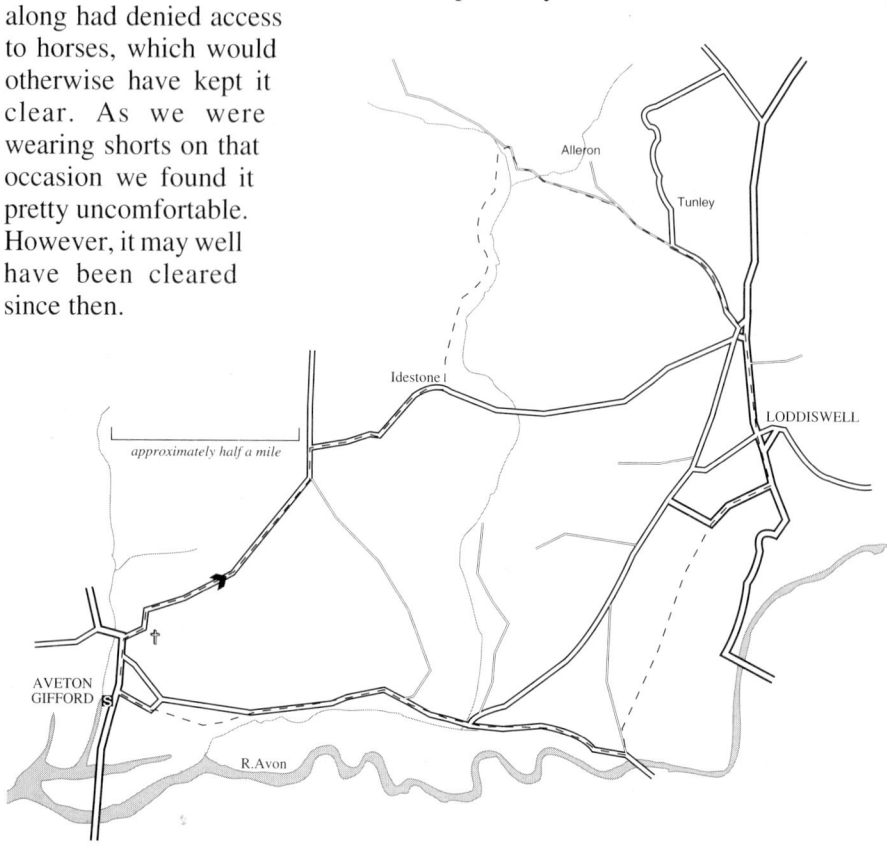

In about three quarters of a mile the bridleway ascends via a rough lane to a hamlet called Idestone. Turn right along the road, which continues to climb for a quarter of a mile to a T-junction. Turn left here, then bear round to the right: this road brings you down into Aveton Gifford in three quarters of a mile, passing the church on the way.

Instead of walking back through the main street as you did on the way out, take the footpath signposted just past the Post Office by the phone box – Townswell Lane. This takes you down an incline to a concrete path between the backs of the houses in the main street and a stream. Cross this by a little bridge just behind the Fishermen's Rest then cross the grass to the underpass into the car park.

Walk Eight

Ivybridge – Ermington

Easy, but a pretty stiff climb of 160 feet at the start. Lanes and footpaths, not too muddy. 5¼ miles. OS 1:50 000 Map 202, OS 1:25 000 Map 1357.

Drive to Ivybridge along the A38 and take the Ermington turning at the mini roundabout at the top of the slip road (fifth exit). Cross the bridge over the A38 and turn left on to the Ermington road. Just after you cross the bridge over the river Erme in about a quarter of a mile, turn sharp left into a cul-de-sac (**not** into the slip road off the A38 which joins here!). There is usually ample parking here, but be careful not to obstruct any entrances, especially that of the fire station.

    The worst part about this walk is the next bit, because you are subjected to the noise and fumes of the traffic on the main road for about half a mile. However, as there is no alternative route we must put up with it. Turn right on to the Ermington road to walk back towards Ivybridge past the sewage works and a small industrial estate. When you reach the T-junction at the end, turn left on to the slip road to the A38 and walk downhill for a couple of hundred yards or so. At the bottom of the hill you will see a lane turning off on your left, which is the road to Westlake. Take this, then start climbing steadily away from the roar of the A38 traffic towards Marjery Cross, which is reached in about three quarters of a mile.

    At Marjery Cross, take the second turning on the left (the first left is a private road down to Cleeve House). The road now levels off for a bit before starting to climb gently to a crossroads (go straight on here, as indicated by the Ermington signpost), then more steeply until you attain a height of 472 feet. There is a television repeater mast here, with glorious views over both southern Dartmoor and the South Hams.

    It's now all downhill to Ermington. Turn left when you come to a T-junction on the outskirts of the village and you will arrive in the village square in a couple of hundred yards. Here you have a choice of pubs: the Crooked Spire, which you come to first, or the First and Last at the other end of the village. The Crooked Spire is so named after the church tower, which, though smaller and less impressive than the one at Chesterfield, nevertheless has the same degree of twist in it, for the same reason: the uneven drying-out of some unseasoned supporting timbers. It looks pretty dodgy, but as it has been like that for centuries it's not about to fall down.

    After lunch, take the short road leading down to the A3121 (ex B3210) half-way between the two pubs. Turn left along the A3121 for a few yards, cross the bridge over the Erme then turn immediately left into a lane running between the river and the Lud Brook. Pass a trout farm and climb up past Strode House. A road joins from the right – just beyond you come to two footpath signs pointing through gateways. We will take the first of these.

approximately half a mile

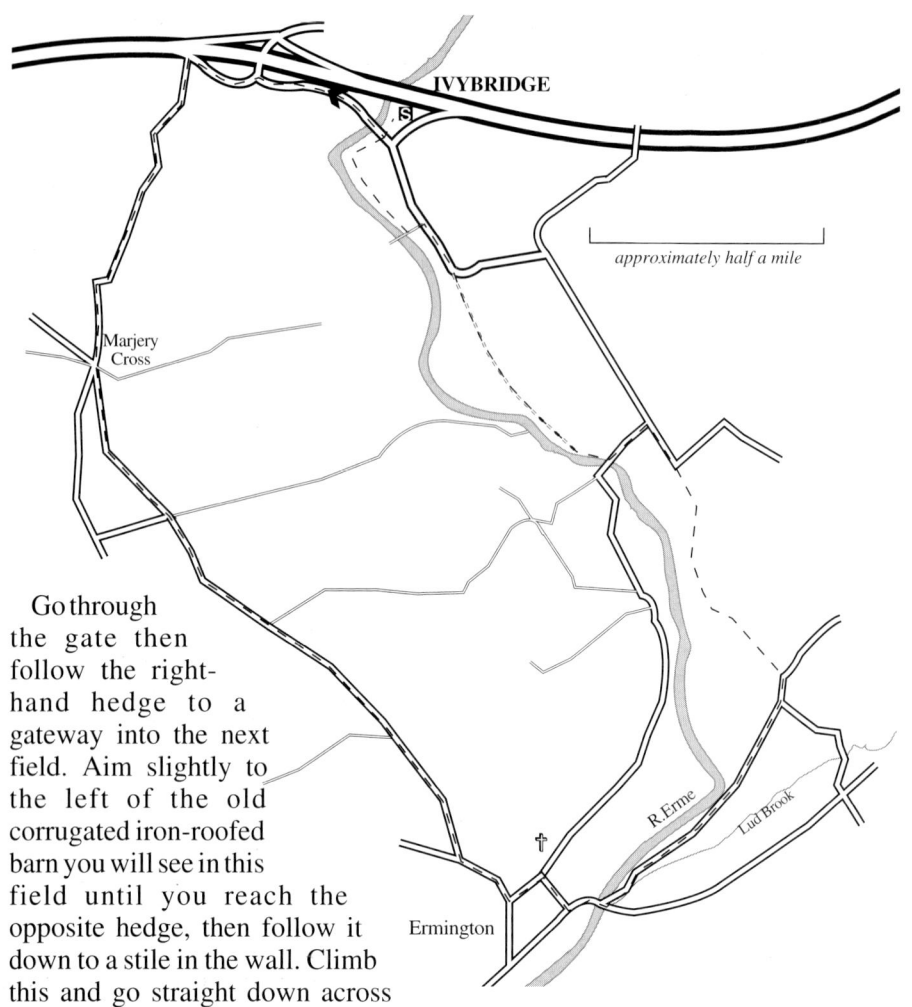

Marjery Cross

IVYBRIDGE

R. Erme

Lud Brook

Ermington

Go through the gate then follow the right-hand hedge to a gateway into the next field. Aim slightly to the left of the old corrugated iron-roofed barn you will see in this field until you reach the opposite hedge, then follow it down to a stile in the wall. Climb this and go straight down across the next field to a gate, which brings you into the end of a lane into an old orchard. Follow the right-hand hedge across this and the next field and you will come to a gate into the road to Penquit Manor. Turn left along the road – you come out on the Ivybridge–Ermington road in a few yards, passing Caton House on your right. Turn left along the Ermington road until you reach Keaton Bridge over the Erme. Just before the bridge a track turns off along the eastern bank of the Erme: a signpost indicates that this leads to a public footpath.

Due to the weir at Keaton, the Erme flows tranquilly here, and it's a good place for fish spotting: mainly brown trout, but sea trout and salmon run up here to spawn in the higher reaches. It's quite a sight to watch them leaping the weirs in a spate.

Eventually you come to a small gate, which is the beginning of the public footpath. From here a track leads across a couple of fields and emerges on to the Ermington road. Go straight on towards Ivybridge on this road for a couple of hundred yards (caution: it's quite busy, and not very wide) until the drive from Cleeve House joins from the left. Go through a gap in the wall into the sports field here, then follow the left-hand hedge down to the river bank. Follow the river upstream to where it makes a right-angle bend. This is Corner Pool, where the sewage works discharges – I'm sure you'll be glad to know that! The huge green blister-like hangar here contains indoor tennis courts. Carry on following the river to the road. A pedestrian underpass by the river takes you under it bringing you out on the road where you parked. This is a bit of the old road, which used to run straight on here and crossed the river via Factory Bridge, which was a homely granite structure, mellow with moss and lichen, which once stood between the two present monstrous concrete bridges.

Walk Nine

Smithaleigh – Lutton

Easy. Along footpaths, bridleways and quiet roads. Muddy in places after rain. 6 miles. OS 1:50 000 Map 202, OS 1:25 000 Maps 1356, 1357.

Turn off the A38 on to the Lee Mill slip road five and a half miles towards Exeter from the Marsh Mills roundabout and flyover at Plymouth, drive down into the village then turn sharp left opposite the Westward Inn up New Park Road. At the top of this road, bear left over the bridge across the A38, then bear right past the New Country Inn and caravan park along the slip road which joins the west-bound A38 eventually. On your left you will come to a long lay-by, a favourite stopping place for HGV drivers and where wide loads await their police escorts. You can park anywhere here, except in the area designated for such wide loads.

Walk back over the bridge over the A38 and take the minor road on the left on the other side, signposted Venton and Cornwood. Walk up past Higher Challonsleigh farm and the turning to Venton on the left. Continue past another turning to Venton, until in one and three quarter miles from your starting point you come to a house with a very prominent arch over the entrance saying "Riverside". Next to this is Mark's Bridge over the Piall River, which runs into the Yealm a few yards downstream. Just beyond this a footpath sign points over a stile on your left. Climb this stile into a wood, then another out of the wood into a field. Proceed to the gate and stile immediately opposite, which take you into another short stretch of woodland before the next gate and stile take you back on to the road. From here you come in a few yards to a turning on your left signposted Venton opposite a house called "Little Stert". Take this turning, and in a couple of hundred yards a Public Bridlepath sign points through a big black wooden gate on your right. Go through this gate and along the path through the woods.

The bridlepath soon emerges from the woods via a gate with a "please shut" notice, then runs along between steep woodland on the left and a level field on the right through which runs the Piall River. It passes under the mightily impressive

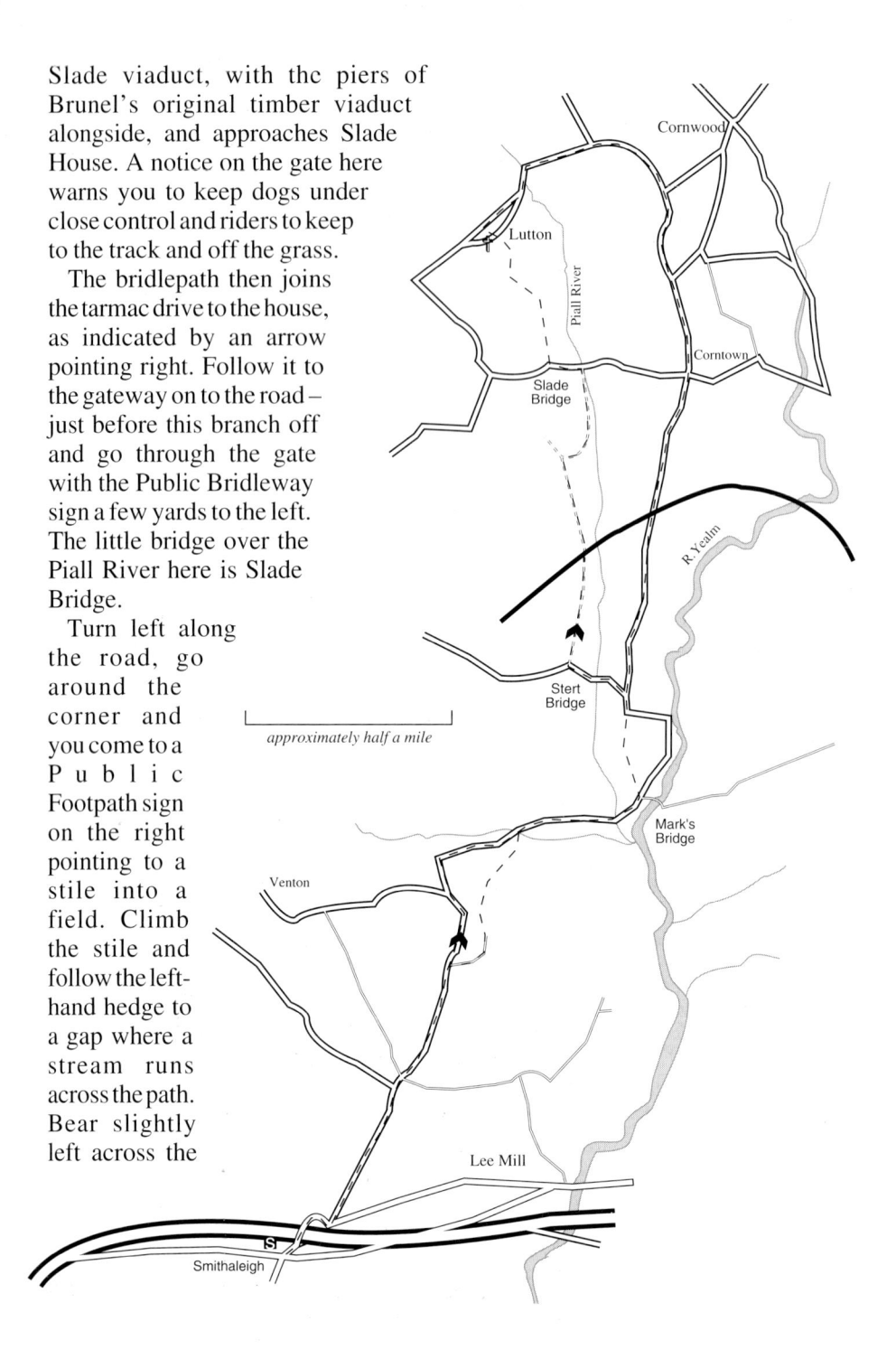

Slade viaduct, with the piers of Brunel's original timber viaduct alongside, and approaches Slade House. A notice on the gate here warns you to keep dogs under close control and riders to keep to the track and off the grass.

The bridlepath then joins the tarmac drive to the house, as indicated by an arrow pointing right. Follow it to the gateway on to the road – just before this branch off and go through the gate with the Public Bridleway sign a few yards to the left. The little bridge over the Piall River here is Slade Bridge.

Turn left along the road, go around the corner and you come to a Public Footpath sign on the right pointing to a stile into a field. Climb the stile and follow the left-hand hedge to a gap where a stream runs across the path. Bear slightly left across the

approximately half a mile

next field to a gateway at the top. Here, where a stream runs under the path, there is a stile on your right. Climb this into the next field.

Cross the very boggy patch in the middle of this field bearing across to the top left-hand corner, where the path used to go through a gate and into a rough little sunken lane leading up to the Cornwood road beside a bus shelter. However, the last time we did this walk major upgrading work was in progress at the sewage works at the bottom of the field, and a new track to take heavy trucks and machinery had been driven straight across this lane and down the field. The footpath had been diverted over a new stile on the left into a new footpath along the edge of the next field and back on to what remains of the old lane.

Cross the Cornwood road to a lane which runs up beside the Methodist Chapel, go up it to the T-junction at the top, turn right and you will come to the Mountain Inn in a few yards, where you can savour your food and drink while basking in the unique atmosphere of this delightful pub.

After lunch you are spared the gruelling climb back up to the moor which we had in Walk Five: turn left outside the pub and descend to the Cornwood road (the road past the pub is the old road). Cross Almshouse Bridge over the Piall River to carry on towards Cornwood, ignoring the turning on your left between the grounds of Delamore House and the local cricket field. Where the road bears sharp left towards Cornwood, turn right opposite Delamore Farm. In about a third of a mile you reach Corntown. Carry straight on at Corntown Cross just beyond, and soon the road begins to widen considerably, it even has a pavement. This is because it used to be the approach to Cornwood station – shortly you will see the old station entrance with its iron railings on your left. The Station House is now a private dwelling.

After this the road narrows again and goes under a railway bridge. In about a third of a mile you will find yourself back at Little Stert. Retrace your steps of earlier in the day along the footpath through the woods to Mark's Bridge, turn right and go back along the road. On your left you pass a sign for a place called "Bryony", and just beyond that a Public Footpath sign indicating a track on the left. Ignore this, go on past "Frog Cottage" and go through the gate on the left indicated by the next Public Footpath sign you come to opposite a house called "Furzedown" (ignore the Public Footpath sign a few yards further on). You can continue on along the road if you wish, but this footpath makes the last leg a little more interesting. Climb up the field following the right-hand hedge to a gate at the top. Go through this and across the next field, still keeping to the right-hand hedge. There is a water-filled ravine on your right. You now enter a track which leads between hedges down to another, more used-looking track. Turn right here past a gate, consisting of a single white-painted steel bar, and a ruined barn to return to the road, where you turn left. The track running on downhill from the gate towards Hitchcombe Farm is **not** a public footpath. Although a path is supposed to run down across the fields to the farm road I wouldn't bother with it: just return along the road past Higher Challonsleigh to the top of New Park Road, cross the bridge over the A38 to return to your car.

Walk Ten

Shaugh Bridge – Clearbrook

Easy. Along the old Plymouth–Launceston railway track (and through a tunnel – it is advisable to take a torch with you), along quiet roads over Roborough Down to Clearbrook, returning by footpaths down the Meavy valley. Not very muddy. Very short, only 4 miles. OS 1:50 000 Map 201, OS 1:25 000 Outdoor Leisure Map 28.

If you are travelling north from Plymouth, turn off the A386 Tavistock road on to the Bickleigh and Shaugh road just beyond the Roborough roundabout, opposite the Plessey factory. Go through Bickleigh village with its Royal Marine Commando camps and continue for another one and a half miles to Shaugh Bridge, where the rivers Plym and Meavy meet. Park in the small parking area just over the bridge. The ruins here are the remains of an old clay "dry": china clay suspended in water was piped down from clay works in the Cadover Bridge area to drying beds, and the resulting clay sludge was finally dried in this building over flues heated by a furnace at one end.

Walk back over Shaugh Bridge, ignore the turning on the right, and carry on along the road towards Bickleigh. Take the next turning right, which leads uphill and crosses the track of the old Plymouth–Tavistock–Launceston branch line by a bridge. However, don't go as far as the bridge: turn off the road to the right through the anti-vehicle barrier on to the old platform of Shaugh Halt, descend to the trackbed, then turn right.

This single-track branch line was extremely picturesque. I travelled it many times while living at Tavistock during World War II, so got to know it well. It succumbed to the Beeching Axe in the sixties, a victim of the increase in private car ownership. It is now a cycle track and footpath.

About 500 yards beyond Shaugh Halt the track enters Leighbeer tunnel. This tunnel curves, so you cannot see daylight at the other end until you are past the half-way stage – it can be pretty dark at this point. As the tunnel is rather wet and there are pools of water on the track, a torch is very handy, although I have walked through without problems when I have forgotten to bring one. However, the main point about carrying a torch is to warn approaching cyclists of your presence!

Shortly after you emerge from the tunnel you come to Goodameavy, where the road over Wigford Down passes under the railway track. It is also the end of the official cycle way, and you leave it via another vehicle-proof barrier for the road just before you get to the bridge. You **can** walk on along the old line to Clearbrook, but houses built across the trackbed prevent access to the village.

Turn right along the road, then climb fairly steeply up to Roborough Down, which you enter via a cattle grid. Follow the road across the Down: at one point you cross a gully which has obviously been scoured out by water. This is the spillway from Drake's leat. The leat is dry most of the time, but was pressed into service to carry away the drainage from Harrowbeer airfield at Yelverton, built during World War II. Although long disused, most of this airfield is still there, still drained by Drake's leat, the water eventually running down to the Meavy via this gully.

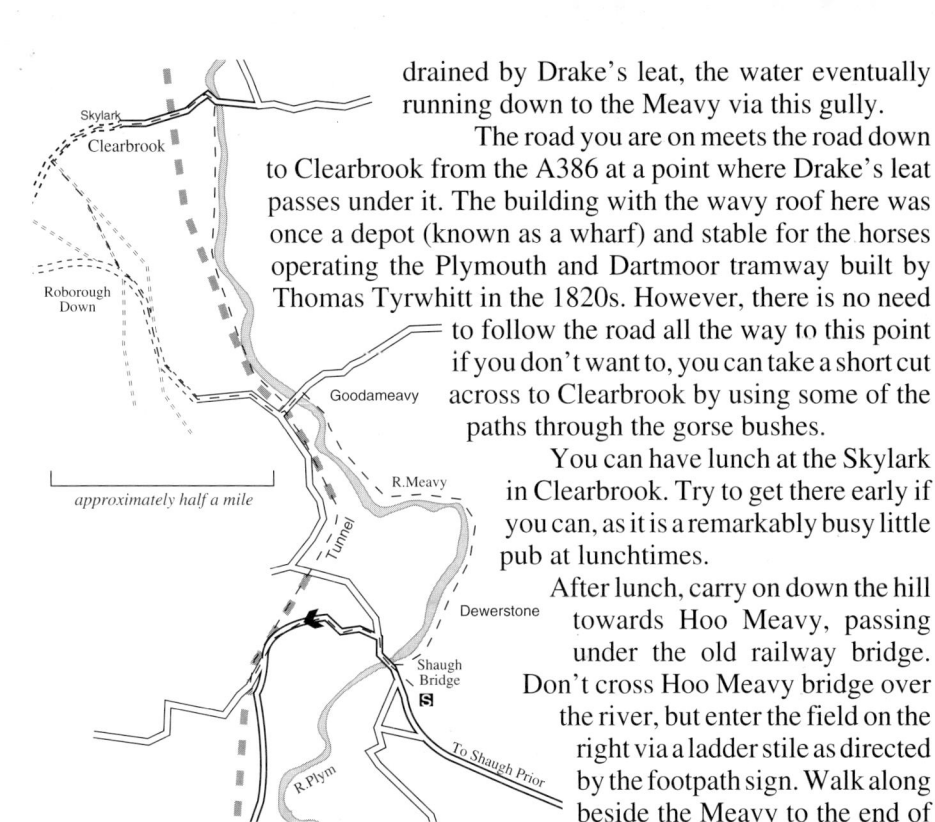

The road you are on meets the road down to Clearbrook from the A386 at a point where Drake's leat passes under it. The building with the wavy roof here was once a depot (known as a wharf) and stable for the horses operating the Plymouth and Dartmoor tramway built by Thomas Tyrwhitt in the 1820s. However, there is no need to follow the road all the way to this point if you don't want to; you can take a short cut across to Clearbrook by using some of the paths through the gorse bushes.

You can have lunch at the Skylark in Clearbrook. Try to get there early if you can, as it is a remarkably busy little pub at lunchtimes.

After lunch, carry on down the hill towards Hoo Meavy, passing under the old railway bridge. Don't cross Hoo Meavy bridge over the river, but enter the field on the right via a ladder stile as directed by the footpath sign. Walk along beside the Meavy to the end of this field. You then enter a short stretch of woodland before emerging into some meadows. Follow the river down through these to a gate leading into the road at Goodameavy, where you left the railway track earlier. Turn left across the bridge over the Meavy, then immediately right through a gate with a National Trust sign just inside.

As you walk along this track you will see over to your right about a quarter of a mile from Goodameavy an embankment and a bridge which look very much as though they once formed part of a railway. The plan was to build a link to the Plymouth–Tavistock line from the Dewerstone quarries via this embankment and a bridge over the river. However, this was never completed.

Eventually you enter woodland and come to Dewerstone Cottage, a base for Scouting activities. You may notice some granite blocks with pairs of holes in them at regular intervals in the track along this stretch: these were the "sleepers" bearing the rails of the quarry tramway. You pass on your left the end of the old inclined plane part of this tramway, from quarries higher up.

Carry straight on along the track, which winds around some striking rock formations before eventually descending by a winding path with steps to Shaugh Bridge. Cross the Meavy via a wooden footbridge to reach the road and return to the car park. This is the latest of a series of bridges: its predecessors were washed away by floods.

OTHER "WALKS" BOOKS

WALKS IN TAMAR AND TAVY COUNTRY, *Denis McCallum*
Another book from the pen (and feet!) of the author of this book. This time Denis explores the countryside of the Rivers Tamar and Tavy – places off the beaten track which are well worth a pedestrian visit.

WALKS IN THE SOUTH HAMS, *Brian Carter*
Written in his own unique style, Brian Carter, presenter of the highly acclaimed "Dartmoor – the Threatened Wilderness", describes some wonderful strolls from around the beautiful South Hams.

WALKING "WITH A TIRED TERRIER" IN AND AROUND TORBAY, *Brian Carter*
Forget the image you may have of Torbay for, like Plymouth, it doesn't take long to find great walking country. Brian Carter is at his very best in this entertaining book.

RAMBLING IN THE PLYMOUTH COUNTRYSIDE, *D. Woolley & M. Lister*
Plymouth is blessed with having some extremely beautiful countryside as its back garden. This books contains a variety of walks on all sides of the city.

TEN FAMILY WALKS ON DARTMOOR, *Sally and Chips Barber*
This is the ideal guide for people who want a gentle baptism to Dartmoor walking. It contains ten walks up to about six miles long and is packed with entertaining facts about the places visited.

TEN FAMILY WALKS IN EAST DEVON, *Sally & Chips Barber*
Written and presented in an identical format, this book explores the driest part of Devon. Ten glorious little walks of up to 5 miles long to savour all that is best in 'sunny' East Devon.

THE TEMPLER WAY, *Derek Beavis*
As the title suggests, this is a guide to the walk that starts at Haytor and finishes at Teignmouth. It is an invaluable guide to an extremely pleasant jaunt through a variety of landscapes.

THE GREAT WALKS OF DARTMOOR, *Terry Bound*
Terry Bound, member of the Long Distance Walking Association, has compiled in this brilliant book all the major walks – Ten Tors, Abbots Way, North-South, OATS walk and many more.

DIARY OF A DARTMOOR WALKER, *Chips Barber*
This is the one book that most Dartmoor enthusiasts will treasure as, written in an amusing and entertaining way, it presents a real picture of Dartmoor, reflecting the trials and tribulations of any avid Dartmoor walker.

DIARY OF A DEVONSHIRE WALKER, *Chips Barber*
This is the sequel to the above mentioned book and includes many more misadventures like the joys of leading an incontinence clinic on a moorland ramble or tripping over courting couples whilst out on evening excursions ... you get the picture? Get the book!